SAVORY and SWEET
SHRUBS

SAVORY and SWEET
SHRUBS

Tart Mixers *for* Delicious COCKTAILS *and* MOCKTAILS

MICHAEL DIETSCH

PHOTOGRAPHY BY BECCA MAFFETT / TERRAGOLD PHOTO

An Imprint of W. W. Norton & Company
Independent Publishers Since 1923

Copyright © 2025 by Michael Dietsch
Photos © by Becca Maffet / Tarregold Photo

All rights reserved
Printed in the United States of America
First Edition

For information about permission to reproduce selections from this book, write to
Permissions, Countryman Press, 500 Fifth Avenue, New York, NY 10110

For information about special discounts for bulk purchases, please contact
W. W. Norton Special Sales at specialsales@wwnorton.com or 800-233-4830

Manufacturing by Versa Press
Book design by Raphael Geroni
Art director: Allison Chi
Production manager: Devon Zahn

Countryman Press
www.countrymanpress.com

An imprint of W. W. Norton & Company, Inc.
500 Fifth Avenue, New York, NY 10110
www.wwnorton.com

978-1-68268-967-7

1 2 3 4 5 6 7 8 9 0

To Jennifer, Julian, and Mirabelle

CONTENTS

9	INTRODUCTION
12	FLAVOR PAIRINGS AND SUBSTITUTIONS
17	SHRUBS—A DEFINITION AND HISTORY
27	PROCESSES, TOOLS, AND TIPS
29	INGREDIENTS

43 Shrubs

44	Apple and Horseradish Shrub
45	Apple, Thyme, and Allspice Shrub
47	Apricot, Basil, and Balsamic Shrub
48	Basil Shrub
49	Banana and Coconut Shrub with Cinnamon and Clove
50	Banana and Pineapple Shrub with Nutmeg
53	Blood Orange, Ginger, and Old Bay Shrub
54	Blueberry, Cinnamon, and Clove Shrub
56	Blackberry and Black Pepper Shrub
57	Cantaloupe, Fennel, and Star Anise Shrub
58	Chamomile, Pear, and Lavender Shrub
59	Carrot and Fenugreek Shrub
61	Carrot, Apple, and Caraway Shrub
62	Cilantro, Lime, and Jalapeño Shrub
65	Coconut and Lemongrass Shrub
66	Cherry and Cocoa Shrub with Cinnamon
67	Coffee Shrub with Raspberry and Thyme
68	Cranberry and Pine Needle Shrub
71	Cucumber, Cilantro, and Coriander Shrub
72	Fennel and Tarragon Shrub
73	Fig, Clove, and Vanilla Shrub
74	Fig and Green Anise Shrub
75	Fire Cider Shrub
79	Green Tea and Ginger Shrub
80	Grape and Rosemary Shrub
81	Habanero, Watermelon, and Thyme Shrub
82	Hibiscus Shrub
85	Honeydew, Fig, and Mint Shrub
86	Lavender Shrub
88	Mango and Basil Shrub
89	Mango and Passion Fruit Shrub with Black Pepper and Mint
91	Meyer Lemon and Za'atar Shrub
92	Mint and Ginger Shrub
93	Olive, Lemon, and Juniper Shrub
94	Oleo-Saccharum
95	Celery and Tarragon Shrub
96	Passion Fruit and Lemon Shrub with Earl Grey Tea
99	Peach and Raspberry Shrub with Cinnamon and Maple
100	Peach and Black Tea Shrub
101	Plum, Orange, and Clove Shrub

102	Pear Shrub with Spiced Molasses Syrup	142	Pinenana Frozen Daiquiri
104	Pomegranate, Grapefruit, and Ginger Shrub	145	Plum Shrub Sidecar
		146	Remember the Day We . . .
106	Papaya and Jalapeño Shrub	147	Rosie Collins
107	Rhubarb and Fennel Shrub	148	Sherry Baby Cobbler
109	Roasted Bell Pepper and Basil Shrub	150	Smashed Hippopotamus
111	Roasted Pineapple and Lime Shrub with Ginger and Turmeric	151	Strawbanero Highball
		153	Tipsy Rabbit
112	Rosemary and Sage Shrub	154	Yuzu Matcha Sour

113 Strawberry and Habanero Shrub
114 Strawberry and Fennel Seed Shrub

157 Mocktails

117 Tart Cherry and Sage Shrub
118 Roasted Sweet Potato Shrub with Turmeric and Garam Masala

159 Agua Fresca
160 Chocolate Coconut Lemongrass Soda

119 Tomato and Dill Shrub
120 Tomato, Cucumber, and Mint Shrub

163 Holiday Cran-Orange Spritzer
164 Honeyfig Julep

123 Watermelon, Cucumber, and Cilantro Shrub

165 Nanacolada
166 Papaya Jalapeño Lassi

124 Yuzu and Matcha Shrub

169 Zingy Ginger Mocktail

127 Cocktails

128 Autumnal Bloody Mary
129 Bowie's Buck

171 ACKNOWLEDGMENTS
172 RESOURCES

131 Bourbon Peach Tea Cooler
132 Chamomile and Pear Toddy

173 FOOD SAFETY TIPS
174 INDEX

135 Fruited Gin and Tonic
136 Good Gourd, Margarita!
137 Olive Shrub Dirty Martini
138 Johnny After a Fashion
141 Nor'easter Winter Punch

Introduction

The beverage we know of today as shrub originated more than 1,000 years ago in Egypt, Turkey, and Persia. Shrub spread from there, first to the west into Europe and then across the Atlantic into colonial America, becoming a favorite nonalcoholic drink during the temperance movement. Shrubs then entered into a deep hibernation after Prohibition.

A rediscovery during the cocktail renaissance of the first decade of this century, however, has taken the shrub worldwide, and it shows no evidence of slumbering again. At the restaurant Stock, in Oslo, you can find a drink called Lack of Faith, with tequila, pineapple shrub, and lime juice. In Dubai, at Bar 44, bartenders mix Monkey Shoulder blended Scotch whisky with a mixed berry shrub and apple and cranberry juices.

At Hero in Nairobi, the Orange Brando features house-made brandy and orange shrub. A riff on the gin and tonic from a bartender in Mumbai features a shrub made from bird's-eye chile and makrut lime leaves.

In Taiwan, you can find a smoky mezcal shrub cocktail with a house-made tarragon shrub and Indian long pepper at Mud Bar at the Amba Taipei Zhongshan Hotel. The Suka Bar in the Fiji Islands offers the Tropical Dream, a tequila sour made with pawpaw shrub, lime, rhubarb, and rosemary. Finally, Rayo Cocktail Bar in Mexico City serves a drink with *raicilla* (an agave spirit), mezcal, and a jackfruit shrub.

As you'll see in the following chapter, early shrubs and their precursors were loaded with herbs, spices, and flowers, from rose water and water lily to nutmeg and fennel seed and even endive. When bartenders and cocktail writers began to rediscover shrubs nearly 20 years ago, most recipes were simple: fruit, sugar, and vinegar. Upon that basic template, however, bartenders and chefs began to layer additional flavors and scents, calling upon a palette of botanicals to liven up the simple shrub.

In the pages that follow, you'll find more than 50 recipes for shrubs inspired by historic and modern bartenders around the world. I've also provided more than 20 examples of ways to incorporate these flavors into cocktails and drinks, both alcoholic and nonboozy.

You can follow these recipes to the letter and I know you'll have great results, but please also feel free to experiment with them. Many fruits, for example, are quite versatile in terms of flavor pairings. I might suggest fennel seed in a recipe where thyme or sage will also perfectly fit, for example. See the table of Flavor Pairings and Substitutions on page 12 for inspiration. Take my suggestions as a jumping-off point for your own explorations. And have fun! That's what this is all about, after all.

Flavor Pairings and Substitutions

Use this flavor pairings table to help explore the wide variety of combinations and pairings. For example, say you want to make an apple shrub. Check the table to see which ingredients pair well with apple, and you might decide, *Oh, an apple shrub with nutmeg and vanilla sounds nice . . .*

MAIN INGREDIENT	COMPLEMENTARY FLAVORS
Apples	Almonds, caramel, cinnamon, earthy spices (allspice, cardamom, cloves, nutmeg), fennel, ginger, pecans, sage, thyme, vanilla, walnuts
Apricots	Almonds, anise, black pepper, cherries, earthy spices, ginger
Bananas	Blueberries, chocolate, coconut, earthy spices, ginger, honey, pineapple
Beets	Apples, basil, black pepper, caraway seeds, dill, horseradish, lemon, tarragon, walnuts
Bell peppers	Basil, black pepper, thyme, tomatoes

Blackberries	Black pepper, chocolate, cinnamon, cloves, vanilla
Blueberries	Cinnamon, earthy spices, ginger, honey, maple syrup, peaches, vanilla
Cantaloupes	Basil, cilantro, raspberries
Carrots	Anise, basil, celery, chile peppers, cinnamon, cumin, dill, ginger, maple syrup, spearmint, tarragon, thyme
Celery	Basil, capers, carrots, tarragon
Cherries	Almonds, apricots, caramel, chocolate, cinnamon, coconut, earthy spices, lemons, vanilla
Coconuts	Almonds, bananas, basil (Italian or Thai), black pepper, chocolate, honey, limes, mangoes, passion fruit, pineapple, vanilla
Cranberries	Apples, apricots, cinnamon, earthy spices, ginger, honey, lemons, maple syrup, orange, vanilla, walnuts
Cucumbers	Basil, bell peppers, black pepper, chile peppers, cilantro, dill, lemons, mint, tomatoes
Dates, fresh or dried	Apples, bananas, caramel, chives, coconut, coffee, maple syrup, oranges, pistachios
Fennel, fresh	Apples, beets, fennel seeds, lemons, mint, olives, oranges, rosemary, thyme, tomatoes
Figs, fresh or dried	Anise, apples, cherries, chocolate, cinnamon, earthy spices, honey, lemons, oranges, pistachios, raspberries, vanilla, walnuts
Ginger, fresh	Apples, basil, chile peppers, chocolate, cilantro, cinnamon, cumin, honey, lemons, mint, molasses, passion fruit, pears, turmeric
Grapefruit	Bananas, caramel, coconut, ginger, honey, mint, pomegranate, tarragon, tomatoes

Flavor Pairings and Substitutions

Grapes	Almonds, cumin, fennel seeds, lemons, pears, rosemary, walnuts
Honeydews	Basil, blackberries, black pepper, coconut, coriander, cumin, ginger, honey, lemons, mint, peaches, red pepper flakes, tarragon
Kiwifruits	Bananas, cherries, chocolate, coconut, hazelnuts, honey, papaya, strawberries
Lemons	Almonds, anise, bananas, basil, bay leaves, berries (of all sorts), black pepper, black tea, capers, caramel, cardamom, cayenne, cinnamon, coffee, ginger, honey, maple syrup, mint, oregano, parsley, poppy seeds, rosemary, thyme, vanilla
Limes	Berries (of all sorts), caramel, chile peppers, cilantro, coconut, ginger, green tea, honey, lemongrass, maple syrup, mint
Mangos	Anise, bananas, basil, bell peppers, berries (of all sorts), caramel, cayenne, chile peppers, cilantro, cinnamon, earthy spices, ginger, mint, pineapple
Oranges	Almonds, anise, bananas, basil, berries (of all sorts), chile peppers, chocolate, cilantro, cinnamon, cranberries, fennel (fresh or seed), ginger, honey, maple syrup, mint, paprika, peaches, pears, rosemary
Peaches and nectarines	Allspice, almonds, anise, basil, bay leaves, berries (of all sorts), caramel, chile peppers, chocolate, cinnamon, coconut, ginger, honey, lemon verbena, maple syrup, mint, nutmeg, pistachios, vanilla
Pears	Almonds, anise, apples, basil, black pepper, borage, caramel, cardamom, celery, chocolate, cinnamon, cloves, ginger, honey, mint, nutmeg, pistachios, rosemary, vanilla
Pineapples	Allspice, bananas, basil, black pepper, caramel, cardamom, chile peppers, chocolate, cilantro, cinnamon, coconut, ginger, honey, star anise, vanilla

Plums	Allspice, anise, bay leaves, cardamom, cinnamon, ginger, honey, juniper berries, lavender, mint, nutmeg, sage, thyme, vanilla
Pomegranates	Allspice, almonds, beets, cardamom, chile peppers, cinnamon, cloves, coriander, cucumbers, cumin, ginger, parsley, turmeric
Pumpkins	Allspice, apples, bay leaves, black pepper, caramel, carrots, cayenne, chile peppers, cilantro, cinnamon, cloves, cranberries, cumin, ginger, mace, marjoram, nutmeg, rosemary, sage, thyme
Raspberries	Chocolate, cinnamon, cloves, ginger, honey, lemon verbena, mint, peaches, pistachios
Strawberries	Almonds, bananas, black pepper, caramel, cardamom, chocolate, cinnamon, coriander, elderflower syrup, ginger, honey, lemon verbena, limes, melons, mint, nutmeg, oranges, vanilla
Tomatilloes	Chile peppers, cilantro, cucumbers, limes, tomatoes
Tomatoes	Basil, bay leaves, bell peppers, black pepper, capers, carrots, cayenne, celery, chervil, chile peppers, cilantro, cucumbers, cumin, fennel (fresh and seeds), marjoram, mint, oregano, paprika, parsley, thyme, watermelons
Watermelons	Anise, basil, berries (of all sorts), black pepper, chili powder, cilantro, cucumber, fennel (fresh and seeds), honey, mint, tomatoes

For much more information on flavor combinations and pairings, I recommend the excellent book *The Flavor Bible,* by Karen Page and Andrew Dornenburg, which lists hundreds of ingredients, alphabetically, and suggests other ingredients to pair with them in dishes and beverages. If you buy, for example, oregano at the farmers' market, and you want to make a shrub with it, you can look up "oregano" in *The Flavor Bible* and find that it pairs well with bell peppers, lemons, and tomatoes.

SHRUBS— A Definition and History

A shrub is nothing more than an acidulated syrup used to make mixed drinks and cocktails.

The word *acidulated*, here, is doing a heavy amount of work. The word itself simply means acidic, or acidified, meaning the drink contains some type of acid. Acidulated beverages are quite common, though we don't normally refer to them with that name. A glass of lemonade is acidulated, of course, with the acidity coming from lemon juice. The mild tartness you may have noticed in Coca-Cola and other sodas comes from phosphoric acid, and the tanginess of these drinks is meant to balance the sweetness.

In shrubs, this acid usually comes in one of two forms: either citric acid from citrus fruits—such as oranges, lemons, or limes—or acetic acid, from vinegar. Historically, two main types of shrubs have been produced: one consists of citric acid, in the form of lemons or Seville oranges, blended with alcohol (typically rum or brandy) and sugar. The other contains acetic acid (vinegar), mixed with fruit juice (or less commonly, vegetable juice) and sugar.

WHAT HAS ANY OF THIS TO DO WITH SHRUBBERY??

I should backtrack for a couple of notes on terminology here: First, shrubs are often referred to as drinking vinegars, and I've probably called them such myself. This, however, isn't entirely accurate because some shrubs contain citrus juice, instead of vinegar, as the acidifying agent.

Second, how is this connected to hedges, bushes, and other small woody plants? It isn't. The English word *shrub* is in actuality two words, unrelated except in spelling and pronunciation, with two different histories and origins.

From Old English we've taken the word *scrybb*, meaning "brushwood." This term evolved into Middle English as *schrobbe*, and eventually into our modern *shrub*, meaning the kind of bushlike, low-rise woody plant, with multiple stems poking out above the ground.

The topic of this book, however, is the beverage bearing the same word. This sense of *shrub* arises from Arabic, namely *sharāb*, which can mean either an alcoholic beverage (namely, wine) or a nonalcoholic beverage, often combining sugar and water flavored with fruits, flowers, or spices. Other terms that derive from *sharāb* include *sherbet*, *sorbet*, and *syrup*.

EVOLUTION OF A SHRUB

A pharmacist's manual from Cairo, from the year 1260, lists several syrups, their ingredients, and their purported medicinal purposes, including rose water julep, thought to soothe bile; *sharāb al-nīlūfar* (water lily syrup), for fevers; *sharāb al-laymūn al-safarjalī*, a syrup of lemon and quince, thought to aid digestion; and *sakanjabīn buzūrī*, a seed-based oxymel, made of dodder seed, fennel seed, celery seed, aniseed, endive seed, vinegar, and sugar, thought to aid the liver and spleen.

Related to shrub is a beverage called *sakanjabīn*, a Persian quaff of vinegar with honey or sugar. The name itself is a compound meaning "vinegar honey"—the Persian *serke* (vinegar) and *angabin* (honey). In English, a beverage of honey and vinegar is referred to as *oxymel*, and again, the word is a compound, this time of words of Greek origin—*oxy* (acid) and *mel* (honey).

These types of syrups were known throughout the medieval Muslim world. In the 1400s, an unknown scribe collated a group of recipes into a volume called *The Book of Cooking in Maghreb and Andalus in the Era of Almohads* (also known as the *Anonymous Andalusian Cookbook*). The recipes come from earlier cookbooks, some dating back to the eighth century CE, and the book compiles the culinary traditions of the Almohad Caliphate, which controlled North Africa, parts of modern-day Spain and Portugal, and Sicily and southern Italy, roughly in the 12th and 13th centuries.

The Andalusian author included syrups made from such roots as fennel, celery, carrot, and chicory, along with such spices as cinnamon, clove, ginger, rhubarb, nutmeg, and saffron, and the book also includes a simple sakanjabīn made of vinegar and either honey or sugar.

In a 14th-century Egyptian cookbook, an anonymous author describes a quince oxymel (*sakanjabīn safarjalī*) with the following recipe: one part by weight of quince juice, a roughly equal portion of sugar, and a quarter the amount of very sour vinegar. Boil these into a thick syrup, and if desired, add thinly sliced pieces of quince. To make a more aromatic version of this, add rose water, saffron, and musk.

The same author describes a quince drink (*sharāb al-safarjal*) made with aged wine, along with honey or sugar, and seasoned with ginger, cassia, cubeb, green cardamom, nutmeg, spikenard, cinnamon, aloeswood, mastic, and saffron.

EUROPEANS DISCOVER SHERBET

Beverages from what we now call the Middle East began to reach European attention in the late 1500s and early 1600s, including a beverage that Europeans knew as *sherbet*. Now, today, we think of sherbet as a frozen dessert, but the drink that European travelers knew in the 17th century was essentially equivalent to the sharabs and sakanjabīns that Persians, Turks, and Egyptians had enjoyed for centuries.

George Sandys, who published early English translations of Ovid, Virgil, and other books of the antiquities, was also an avid traveler, visiting Virginia in the early years of the American colony and then Turkey, where he encountered sherbet, which he described in a 1615 book as being made of lemon juice and sugar, occasionally with violets.

In 1625, an English cleric named Samuel Purchas published a travelogue called *Purchas His Pilgrimes*, a book detailing not his own travels, but accounts passed along to him from other wanderers. One section discusses the foods and drinks served in the royal court of the Ottoman Empire in the early 1600s, and writes of sherbet being served on snow, a precursor to today's frozen sherbets.

Nearly a decade later, in 1634, Thomas Herbert, a nobleman who traveled the world and served as a courtier to King Charles I, published a book of his travels to Africa and Asia, including accounts of his stay in Persia, where he encountered public houses in which Persians drank wine, arrack (a grape-based distilled beverage, somewhat like an unaged brandy), sherbet, and another beverage just beginning its ascendance: coffee. Of sherbet, he writes that it contains water, rose water, sugar, and lemon juice.

Another nobleman, Henry Blount, traveled into the same region at about the same time and recounted drinking sherbets made of sugar, lemon juice, peaches, apricots, violets or other flowers, and plums.

It wasn't long before sherbet arrived in Europe itself, and by the 17th century, it had caught on in Venice, which was at the time a prosperous trading center between Western Europe and the Islamic world. Venetian traders imported ginger and pepper from the Indian subcontinent, cinnamon from today's Sri Lanka, hemp from Syria, cotton and cloves from Egypt, and nutmeg from Malaysia. Venetian ships exported wine, paper, earthenware, and glass.

Within a few decades, sherbet was all the rage in London. The third edition (1797) of the *Encyclopedia Britannica* contains an entry for sherbet, naming it "a compound drink, first brought into England from Turkey and Persia, consisting of water, lemon juice, and sugar, in which are dissolved perfumed cakes made of excellent Damascus fruit, containing an infusion of some drops of rose water."

FROM SHERBET TO SHRUB

Up to this point, *shrub* was simply an alternative way to render the word *sherbet*, but at some point seemingly around the year 1700, shrub took on an ingredient lacking in sherbet: alcohol, in the form of either brandy or rum. Sherbet, being a beverage enjoyed in Muslim societies, was necessarily nonalcoholic, since Islam prohibits the consumption of intoxicants.

In 1705, a book appeared in London called *The Pastry-Cook's Vade Mecum*. The term *vade mecum* comes from Latin and simply means a pocket-size how-to manual. The anonymous author offers a recipe for "an excellent Liquor called shrub": Take two quarts of brandy and five thinly sliced lemons picked of their seeds, and stopper that up for five days. Strain out the lemons, and then add white wine, water, and sugar. Stir until the sugar dissolves, and then strain and bottle it.

A 1729 book, *The Compleat Housewife*, by Eliza Smith, contains a similar recipe: Pour two quarts of brandy into a large bottle. Add the juice of five lemons, the peels of two, and half a nutmeg. Stopper that up and let it stand for three days. Add white wine and sugar, and then strain and bottle it.

Not much is known of Eliza Smith, aside from the fact that she was a housekeeper for 30 years. Her book, however, was quite popular, with 18 editions. *The Compleat Housewife* is also noteworthy as the first cookery book sold in the Thirteen Colonies of what would become the United States, printed in Williamsburg, Virginia, in 1742.

Shrub itself, however, arrived on the shores of North America decades sooner. In 1716, Alexander Spotswood, the royal governor of Virginia, led an expedition called the Knights of the Golden Horseshoe up the Rappahannock River to explore the Blue Ridge Mountains. One of his officers was a gentleman named James Taylor; among *his* great-grandchildren were two future US presidents, James Madison and Zachary Taylor.

In his history of Virginia published in 1860, historian Charles Campbell wrote that Spotswood's intrepid crew "had with them a large number of riding and packhorses, an abundant supply of provisions, and an extraordinary variety of liquors." I'll say! This "variety" included "Virginia red wine and white wine, Irish usquebaugh [whiskey], brandy, shrub, two kinds of rum, champagne, canary [a sweet wine from the Canary Islands], cherry punch, cider, etc."

THE RELATIONSHIP BETWEEN SHRUB AND PUNCH

At some point, shrub became an ingredient in punch. When? No one knows, but that's okay, because no one really knows when punch itself was invented either. Punch, and by this I mean the classic punch that arose some time prior to 1700, is an interesting beast, much more complex than the stuff people mix into large metal tubs and serve at college parties.

Punch took many forms in its early days; it could be served hot or cold, depending on circumstances. A hot punch kept warm by a roaring fire in a northern English tavern during deepest winter has as much appeal as an iced punch served in the Caribbean in brightest summer. Punches of the time often had a spirit, such as rum or brandy, as its base, though the main ingredient was also frequently wine, and to complicate the matter further, the base could be a mix of liquor and wine.

Punch contained water to stretch the beverage and to dilute it so that it wouldn't inebriate the drinker immediately. And punches often contained some kind of spicy ingredient, sometimes nutmeg, though teas could also be used in this capacity.

Finally, early punches weren't punches at all without some sort of citrus component . . . and this is where shrub comes in.

In 1736, the lexicographer Nathan Bailey published one of the earliest English dictionaries, the *Dictionarium Britannicum*, where he describes shrub as a "compound of brandy, the juice of [Seville] oranges and lemons kept in a vessel for the ready making of punch at any time, by the addition of water and sugar."

This was, however, just one way to make shrub. In his 2010 book *Punch*, spirits historian David Wondrich describes shrubs for punch-making as containing sugar and citrus juice, often with the booze added as well. Either way, shrub was an ingredient for punch-making, kept ready for purposes of revelry.

SHRUB AND THE SEVEN SEAS

Around the same time that Bailey was writing, a 1737 document called the *Historical Register* noted a duty levied in New York on the importation by ship of rum, brandy, and shrub. Fifteen years later, a New York law book references other duties and tariffs imposed on the importation of liquors and shrub.

In October 1747, *Gentlemen's Magazine* published a long piece, written anonymously, entitled "A Method for Preserving the Health of Seamen in Long Cruises and Voyages." The writer laments the loss of "vast numbers of sailors" to the disease of scurvy, sadly common in those days on long sea voyages.

Scurvy is caused by a deficiency of ascorbic acid (vitamin C) in the diet. Vitamin C is crucial because it helps make collagen, without which tissue begins to break down. Symptoms include anemia, bleeding gums and loosened teeth, skin hemorrhages, and wounds that don't heal, leading to infections.

The condition is rare today, because we mostly get more than enough vitamin C, but especially on sea voyages, it was a serious illness with grave consequences. Any shipowners who lost a few profitable trading voyages to a vessel full of dead crewmen would rapidly start seeking solutions. Luckily, the advantages of eating fresh fruits and vegetables were commonly understood, even if the concept of vitamins weren't.

The anonymous author notes that ships carrying apples (and apple cider), lemons, and oranges saw impressive results in preventing scurvy. What the writer proposes, therefore, is provisioning ships with barrels of cider and fresh fruit. If this is impractical, he writes, "a mixture of lemon juice and rum (shrub as they call it) may be carried in any quantity, as it will keep a long time."

(An interesting sidenote here: Although sailors of the time understood that they could prevent scurvy by consuming apples and citrus, what no one yet knew was the role of vitamin C; they knew that consuming fruit worked, they just didn't understand why or how. Vitamin C, itself, wasn't discovered until 1912.)

Throughout the 18th century, sailing literature is replete with exhortations to carry citrus or shrub, and also accounts of citrus or shrub in a ship's hold. Also common in this era were recipe books containing methods for making shrubs, often from a liquor, such as brandy or rum, the juices and peels of either lemons or Seville oranges, and sugar. Shrub in this era was common and popular among both seamen and landlubbers alike.

SHRUB IN THE NINETEENTH CENTURY

Throughout the 1800s, a number of cookery books and literary accounts continue to document the popularity of rum or brandy shrubs, made with citrus juice and sugar. A Mrs. Hannah Glasse brings us such a recipe in her *The Compleat Confectioner* of 1800. Nearly 30 years later, in 1827, an Irishman named Sir Jonah Barrington laments in his memoirs that many of his compatriots have fallen afflicted with gout after too many helpings of rum shrub.

In the 1850s, a newspaper in Honolulu published advertisements touting the availability of rum shrub alongside brandy, rum, gin, and Champagne. Up into the 1880s, rum shrub was still commonly served in hotel barrooms in Manhattan.

Alongside the brandy and rum shrubs, however, the beverage was beginning to tack in another direction. In 1804's *The New Practice of Cookery, Pastry, Baking, and Preserving*, two Scottish writers—named only as Mrs. Hudson and Mrs. Donat—published a recipe for Raspberry Vinegar: Fill a jar with raspberries, cover them with vinegar, and let this stand for 24 hours. Strain it off and then add sugar to the liquid left behind.

Boil it until the sugar dissolves, and then bottle and cork it up tightly.

Recipes for raspberry vinegar proliferate after this. Cookbooks from 1817, 1822, the 1830s, the 1840s, and pretty much every decade up into the 1890s contain essentially the same formula for raspberry vinegar: combine raspberries, sugar, and vinegar.

During this period, too, some writers began to promote supposed health benefits of raspberry vinegar. In 1817, a doctor named William Kitchiner called it "a most excellent cooling beverage to assuage thirst in fevers and colds." In an era when many pharmacologists published their own formularies for medical substances, a man named Samuel Frederick Gray published a recipe for raspberry vinegar. Writers who penned books and articles offering medical advice suggested raspberry vinegar for ailments ranging from measles and sore throat to sleep disorders and "complaints in the chest."

THE BIRTH OF THE SHRUB AS WE KNOW IT

The first writer to use the word *shrub* the way this book conceives of it—as a mixture of fruit, vinegar, and sugar—was probably Lydia Maria Child, in her 1829 book *Frugal Housewife*. A woman of colossal achievement, Child was a novelist, essayist, journalist, and poet, who wrote to advocate the abolition of slavery and the rights of women and Native Americans.

How did this linguistic shift happen? Unclear. One thing that's certain is that it was both expensive and difficult to import citrus into most parts of North America. Early settlers, both Spanish and English, introduced fruit trees (primarily in the form of seeds and seedlings) when establishing their settlements. Oranges took hold in Florida and South Carolina, while New England and the mid-Atlantic colonies saw the introduction of apples, cherries, peaches, and plums. Spanish missionaries brought oranges, olives, figs, and grapes to California and western Texas.

Transporting citrus into the northern colonies was no easy feat. Vinegar, however, could be made with whatever you had on hand, including apples, which were remarkably abundant in the new nation. The simplest and probably most accurate explanation is that Americans retained the familiar word *shrub*, while switching the acid from citrus to vinegar.

Some recipes of the time retain brandy or rum, but as you examine the culinary literature of the 19th century, you see the temperance movement starting to take hold after about 1870, and fewer recipes featuring any kind of alcohol in the shrub whatsoever.

Two cookbooks from Ohio bear out this point. The 1873 *Presbyterian Cook Book*, from a church in Dayton, contains a shrub recipe calling for brandy. This is the very same year that the Women's Christian Temperance Union was organized in Hillsboro, just 60 miles away, and the same year the WCTU succeeded in closing drinking establishments in Washington Court House, Ohio. Perhaps not coincidentally, 1880's *Buckeye Cookery* features only a temperate shrub, made with cider vinegar.

Shrubs continued in popularity throughout the temperance movement and the Prohibition era. In 1903, *Good Housekeeping* wrote: "Gooseberry shrub makes a delicious 'winey' temperance drink." In 1920, a cook named Bertha Stockbridge wrote a cocktail book aimed at the Prohibition market, with recipes for nonalcoholic fruit punches, cocktails, and juleps; shrubs and other fruit syrups; and milk-based drinks.

Numerous American newspapers of the time ran recipes for shrubs alongside advertisements for establishments selling them. "When Will comes up to see me I always make him old-fashioned raspberry shrub. To make this you wash and strain the berries, leaving the juice for five or six days until fermentation has taken place. Then skim the scum from the top and pour off the clear juice carefully, being certain that none of the sediment is in the liquid. Cook it quickly with one and a half pounds of sugar to one pound of juice. Boil in the oven two minutes. Skim, and when cool, pour into bottles. This shrub will keep all year round." This recipe comes from Adelia Torrey and ran in syndication in 1910. The "Will" she mentions is her nephew, President William Howard Taft.

Papers throughout the country ran recipes, advertisements, or other mentions of raspberry and other fruit shrubs, including papers in Nome, Alaska (*Nome Daily Nugget*; May 27, 1911); Bryan, Texas (*Daily Eagle and Pilot*; September 30, 1916), Lucy, Louisiana (*Le Meschacébé*; June 22, 1918), Central City, Colorado (*Gilpin Observer*; January 9, 1919), and El Centro, California (*Imperial Valley Press*; August 26, 1932), plus papers in New Mexico, Minnesota, Indianapolis, Philadelphia, Washington State, and Washington, DC.

SHRUB EBBS AND FLOWS

By the end of Prohibition, however, shrub was on its way out. The drink was a popular temperance beverage for the same reason its antecedent, sherbet, was popular among Muslims: it was alcohol-free. But a compelling new beverage was making great strides during (and because of) the temperance movement and Prohibition: Coca-Cola, the brainchild of Georgia druggist John Pemberton, which came to market in the 1880s. By the early 20th century, teetotalers could buy Coke and its derivatives at soda fountains or in bottles across the country. Why make shrub when you can buy Coke?

Next, shrub was popular among householders as a great way to keep fruit from spoiling; sugar, alcohol, and vinegar are all preservatives. Once refrigeration and canned and frozen fruit came along, however, using vinegar or booze to preserve fruit was no longer necessary.

Finally, once the world's navies realized they could provide vitamin C via canned fruit and juice, daily supplements, and other convenient sources, it was no longer necessary to haul around barrels of shrub everywhere.

Shrub's day wasn't yet over, though it came pretty close. What saved shrub was the ethnic group we know as the Pennsylvania Dutch. As raspberry and other fruit vinegars became popular in colonial America, among the colonials who enjoyed the drink were the Pennsylvania Dutch. However, they had one characteristic missing among other Americans of the 20th century; the Pennsylvania Dutch have preserved most of their food traditions, including shrub.

And it was thanks in huge part to one particular family of Pennsylvanians that we are in the midst of a shrub renaissance today. In July 1986, a farmer named David Tait had a bumper crop of raspberries; unfortunately, however, it was raining torrentially at harvest time, and no one was driving to David's roadside farm stands to buy berries . . . or much of anything else. He picked all the berries and froze them for winter sales. However, he still had too many.

A family friend, Betty Groff, was a cookbook author who had chronicled the Amish and Mennonite culinary traditions of Pennsylvania. Her 1974 book *Good Earth & Country Cooking* (cowritten with José Wilson) featured Raspberry Shrub in a section called Memory Foods. She handed down her recipe for Raspberry Shrub to David Tait, and though I doubt I can say shrubs were an overnight success for the Tait family, they now offer 20 varieties at their farm and online.

SHRUB RENAISSANCE

The person I credit most with sparking a modern worldwide interest in shrubs is Eric Felten, a journalist and author, who in 2006 was writing a drinks column for the *Wall Street Journal*. He wrote a piece one summer on beverages for Independence Day cookouts. Seems that Felten had recently discovered shrubs on a menu at City Tavern in Philadelphia and concluded that their bracing tartness was the perfect thirst-quencher for a hot July weekend. He provided a recipe but then asked, why bother, when you can just buy them from Tait Farms?

Felten's column was always droll and impeccably reported, and given that he was writing during the craft-cocktail movement of the naughts, cocktail nerds like myself eagerly awaited every installment. We immediately began buzzing among ourselves about how to order and make shrubs and shrub cocktails.

The internet being the internet, the idea of shrubs began to spread without stopping, and soon it seemed every mustachioed mixologist was tinkering with them.

Processes, Tools, and Tips

Before we start making shrubs, I should offer a few words about how to go about things, what items to have on hand, and how to store your finished shrubs.

PROCESSES

I generally use either of two different processes for making shrubs—a hot process or a cold process. In the hot process, you make a syrup by cooking it on the stovetop; whereas in the cold process, you make the syrup by steeping fruit and sugar in a bowl, until the sugar draws out the fruit's juice and combines with it to form a syrup.

The hot process is generally faster than the cold. You can make syrup on the stovetop in under an hour; the cold process, however, can take days while you wait for the sugar to do its work. (This is a passive process, though; it happens while you're working or watching Netflix or going for a swim.)

The advantage of the cold process is that it produces a fresher-tasting shrub. Because the cold process doesn't cook the fruit, it leaves more of the flavors of the fruit to shine through. I've tried making shrubs from the same fruit—raspberries—both hot and cold, and I've found that the cold process produces a shrub that tastes like fresh raspberries, whereas the hot process yields a product that tastes like stewed fruit.

I don't mean to imply that I never use the hot process. Sometimes, I want a shrub that tastes like stewed fruit or like a pie baked in the oven. Usually when I choose the hot process for a recipe, I'll explain my choice in the recipe's introduction.

Extracting flavor from herbs and spices requires some explanation. In a hot process, this is pretty easy. You can just add the herb or spice to the cooking pot along with everything else and allow heat to do the work. If you're making a cold-process shrub, though, you need a different technique. In the case of grated or powdered spices, you can mix them with the fruit (or vegetable) and sugar, and it'll be fine.

In other cases, such as most dried spices, sugar won't really extract anything, and you need instead to steep the spices in vinegar, usually at the same time you're macerating the fruit with sugar. For example, in the recipe for Apricot, Basil, and Balsamic Shrub (page 47), the instructions call for macerating apricot and sugar in one container, and steeping basil in balsamic vinegar in another. Then, you strain and combine the ingredients.

TOOLS

One nice thing about shrub-making is that it doesn't require many specialized tools. Some shrubs in this book require being cooked on a stovetop; a few require roasting ingredients in the oven. Some need a blender, but in other cases, you can get away with a box grater. Otherwise, you'll need a citrus squeezer, knives to play with, mesh strainers, a funnel or two, a whole bunch of jars or bottles, and probably a way to label your shrubs (masking tape and a marker or pen are fine).

For the cocktails and mocktails, you'll need a cocktail shaker or another vessel for mixing drinks. A cocktail strainer helps, and maybe a bar spoon. You'll want measuring cups or jiggers. But again, this is nothing too specialized, and you should be able to find all of it easily and without much expense at a kitchen store or online.

STORAGE AND SAFETY TIPS

Storing shrubs in the refrigerator is perfectly safe, for up to one year. However, before serving them, always check them carefully. Look for signs of mold, yeast, or other microbes. If it's moldy, trash it. If you see bubbles, cloudiness, or slime, it's probably fermenting, and you don't want that. (Some shrubs, however, settle over time, as gravity pulls particulates to the bottom of the container. This is normal for many shrubs, and it's perfectly safe. Simply shake the container, and it will be fine.)

Ingredients

Okay, you've read up on the history of shrubs, contemplated the joys of drinking acid, sharpened your knives, unearthed your box grater, and dusted off your blender. Now, it's time to shop! You'll need fruit, vegetables, spices and herbs, vinegars, and two or three types of sweetener.

THE PRODUCE SECTION

Shrub-making might have started as a way to preserve fruit, but the process has branched out to include vegetables and fresh herbs as well. The recipes here are just a beginning, but a basic rule of thumb is, if you can find it at a farmers' market or produce aisle, you can shrub it.

Berries

Berries are possibly the heart and soul of much modern shrub-making. If you shop for commercial shrubs, you'll see countless offerings based on berries, and if you search online for shrub recipes, berry shrubs will be in the first listings. Plus, the flavors of berry shrubs are versatile when it comes to mixing, because they'll blend with nearly any spirit you can imagine, as well as lower-alcohol beverages, such as sherry, port, vermouth, and many bitter, fruity, or herbal liqueurs. Finally, berries are excellent choices for nonalcoholic drinks because they're bright and colorful and full of familiar scents and flavors.

Berries are often available year-round in most American groceries, and though I love buying berries in season from farmers' markets, I think that grocery-store berries bought in, say, February, also make great shrubs. Look for berries that are plump and fragrant and that release juice easily when you squeeze them. Make sure they have no obvious mold on them.

Frozen berries also work beautifully in shrubs; just make sure to thaw them first according to package directions. Whether fresh or frozen, I usually make berry shrubs using the cold process, unless I specifically want to mimic, say, the flavor of pie filling.

Pome Fruit

A pome is a type of fruit with a central inedible core containing multiple small seeds—think: apple, pear, and quince. I usually use a box grater to shred these fruits before steeping them with sugar to make a syrup, though cutting them up into small pieces works well, too. Many farmers' markets and farm stands sell "seconds," which are fruits or vegetables that have bruises or other cosmetic damage. Their prices are marked down, and though you wouldn't want them on your table as fruit to eat out of hand, they're perfect for shrub-making.

Stone Fruit

Stone fruits are specimens that have an outer fleshy part and a pit in the center. Peaches, plums, olives, cherries, and mangoes are all types of stone fruit, and they all pair well with herbs and spices in shrubs. Ask around at the farmers' market; you might find stands with seconds, and they'll save you some money. I'm a bit more likely to use a hot process for stone-fruit shrubs, as plums and cherries, for example, taste great when cooked down a bit, as they are in pies.

Citrus

I must admit to feeling a little envious of my friends who live in warmer climates than Maryland, where I live, and who can reach out their back door and pick a lemon off a tree. I'm unlikely to ever regularly shop for citrus at a farmers' market, but that's fine. I can find most of what I need for shrub-making at my grocery.

Some citrus fruits such as Eureka lemons, Persian limes, and navel oranges are available year-round, whereas others, such as blood oranges, Sumo Citrus (a variety of satsuma mandarins, also known as *dekopon* or Top Knot mandarins), and Meyer lemons, are seasonal.

Tropical Fruits

Fruits that grown in warm equatorial climates are known as tropical fruits, though this classification overlaps with other categories of fruit—for example, much citrus is tropical, though not all tropical fruit is citrus. Tropical fruits include açaí palms, bananas, cacao pods, coconuts, coffee cherries, dragon fruits (pitayas), guavas, jackfruits, lychees, mangoes, papayas, passion fruits, pineapples, and tamarinds, among many others. Although grocery stores usually carry pineapples and bananas year-round, many other tropical fruits are available only seasonally.

Frozen, Precut, Dried, or Canned Fruit

Often, it's hard to find certain fruits in their fresh, whole form. For example, fresh cranberries are frequently only available in the fall, near Thanksgiving, whereas you can find frozen cranberries year-round. Using frozen fruit in shrubs is perfectly fine; simply follow the package directions for thawing them before use.

Also, your grocery store might have precut pineapple, melon, or coconut available in the produce section, just feet away from whole specimens. These are also great conveniences to use in shrub-making.

Shredded or dried coconut is also just fine for shrubs; simply steep it in vinegar for a day or two to infuse its flavor.

However, I advise against most canned fruit. The canning process cooks the fruit and removes much of its flavor. As a result, much canned fruit is preserved in syrup, which keeps it moist but also adds a lot of sugar. Avoid it.

Bottled Juices

Bottled juices, especially those that are freshly squeezed and available in a refrigerated area of the produce section, might seem like convenient substitutes for fresh fruit. I tend to avoid them, though, unless it's impossible to find fresh items or unless the fresh stuff is simply a pain to make juice from. (Yes, I'm talking to you, pomegranate.)

Fruit Vegetables

Do you know that a tomato is a fruit, not a vegetable? Of course, you do. Do you know that's also true of bell and chile peppers, cucumbers, eggplants, peas, pumpkins, and zucchini? Botanically speaking, a fruit develops from the flower of a plant and contains seeds, whereas the remaining parts of the plant—the roots, bulbs, stems, and leaves—are considered vegetables.

Culinarily, however, fruits and vegetables are distinguished by taste. Fruits are sweet or tart, whereas vegetables are savory or mild. Fruits can be part of a dessert or sweet snack, whereas veggies are ingredients in main courses, side dishes, savory snacks, or salads.

For shrub-making, I feel that fruit vegetables (the fruits we use as vegetables) are best when they're seasonal. After all, it's hard to find a great tomato in February.

Vegetables

Real vegetables! Vegetable vegetables! Carrots, celery, beets, fennel, and rhubarb all make for magnificent shrubs. I prefer to buy them at farmers' markets simply because I feel that the more local they are, the fresher they're likely to taste.

Herbs and Spices

As the term *herb* is commonly used, it refers to the leafy or flowering parts of a plant (either fresh or dried) that are used to flavor or garnish foods. Spices are used for the same purposes, but consist of the dried portions of other parts of the plant, including the roots, seeds, or bark.

For the purposes of this book, I've grouped some ingredients in this category that technically are vegetables—namely, horseradish, ginger, and turmeric, which are generally used culinarily in the same way one uses herbs and spices, as flavoring agents instead of main ingredients.

TEAS AND HERBAL TEAS

Teas and herbal teas are beverages made by infusing fresh or dried plant parts, such as leaves, in hot water. These pair deliciously with fruit to make complex shrubs. Tea, technically, refers to leaves, leaf buds, or stems of *Camellia sinensis*, a plant cultivated in tropical and subtropical regions. Green tea and black tea are both made from *Camellia sinensis*. Common tea varieties include Darjeeling, which is a geographic designation for *Camellia sinensis* cultivated from the Darjeeling or Kalimpong district in India. English breakfast tea is a combination of black teas from India, Sri Lanka, and Kenya, blended to pair well with milk and sugar.

Flavored teas are usually black teas blended with fruit, spices, or herbs, such as apple or cinnamon. Earl Grey tea is a flavored tea, made with black tea blended with oil of bergamot, a type of citrus fruit. Mint tea can be either black tea flavored with mint leaves or simply dried (or fresh) mint leaves steeped in hot water. Check the ingredient label to be sure. Lapsang souchong is a Chinese variety of *Camellia sinensis,* smoked and dried over a pinewood fire.

Redbush, also known as rooibos, is a reddish-brown tea made from *Aspalathus linearis,* a plant that grows in South Africa. Rooibos contains no caffeine and has a sweet, nutty, woody taste.

I don't have any recipes in this book that call for Lapsang or rooibos, but feel free to experiment if you're curious. Lapsang's flavor reminds many of smoky Scotch whisky or mezcal. Smoky flavors pair really well with many fruits, such as apple, plum, cherry, berry, or with such vegetables as bell peppers or carrots. The woody flavors of rooibos sound delicious with peaches or pears.

> ✻ **SAFETY NOTE:** To prevent future growth of microorganisms on fruit, vegetables, and herbs, you can sanitize them in a vinegar-water solution. Prepare a pot or pan or large bowl by adding 1 tablespoon of distilled white vinegar to 6 cups of water. Soak fruit, vegetables, or herbs in the solution for 10 minutes, drain, and then rinse.

SUGARS AND OTHER SWEETENERS

You'll find that most recipes in this book use either of two sweeteners—granulated white cane sugar or turbinado (sold commercially as Sugar in the Raw). These sugars are reliable, relatively inexpensive, and easy to find. By *reliable*, I mean they work consistently well in any recipe. However, if you want to branch out into your own shrub-making, you might want to try other sugars, which I'll discuss later.

The role of sugar in shrub-making is twofold. In a basic cold-process shrub, sugar steeps with fruit and draws out juice; it then mingles with the juice to form a syrup. When you then mix the syrup with vinegar, the sugar balances out the tartness of the vinegar.

Most sugar you'll find is the product of either sugarcane or sugar beets, though specialty markets often also sell sugars made from palm, coconut, date, and maple. Cane sugar is the least expensive and most widely available of these types, with nearly 80 percent of refined sugar coming from cane.

Types of Cane Sugar and How It Is Refined

Sugar is a naturally occurring carbohydrate, produced during photosynthesis to provide energy to plants. When most folks think of refined white table sugar—the stuff used in coffee or baking—they're thinking of cane sugar, which derives from sugarcane, one of humanity's oldest foods. Sugarcane is a tall, perennial grass grown in tropical and subtropical climates. Production in the United States centers on Florida, Louisiana, and Texas. Sugarcane, like shrub itself, arrived in Europe and the Americas via the Middle East, namely Egypt and Cyprus. The word *sugar* derives from the Arabic *al-sukar*.

Sugar refining is a complex process, requiring complicated machinery and techniques, and describing the process is beyond the scope of this book, but essentially, sugarcane is crushed or shredded and then milled to extract the sugary juice of the cane. This liquid is heated to evaporate water from the juice and concentrate the sugar, causing crystals to appear. As the juice is boiled down to concentrate the sugar, a dark syrup results: molasses.

Refined white sugar has all the molasses stripped out. Natural brown sugar retains some of the molasses, whereas refined brown sugar has molasses added back to refined white sugar. Some types of natural brown sugar include turbinado, Demerara, and muscuvado. These three are largely interchangeable in shrub-making, but I call for turbinado because it's the most widely available.

Other Sweeteners

Many other sweeteners are useful for shrub-making, though I generally stick to turbinado or granulated sugar. The choice of which sweetener to use depends largely on which flavor profile you're going for when developing your recipe. Some ingredients lend themselves well to maple flavors, either from maple sugar or pure maple syrup (though please don't use artificially flavored pancake syrup). Some recipes seem to cry out for honey or agave nectar. You can even use molasses, which imparts a grassy funk to shrubs, though you need to be careful so the molasses doesn't overpower the other flavors. Generally, maple syrup, honey, agave nectar, and molasses work best in hot-processed shrubs, because you need the heat to melt them down enough to blend with other ingredients.

VINEGAR

Vinegar is the natural result of ongoing fermentation, a process in which microorganisms, such as yeast and bacteria, transform sugar into alcohol (ethanol) and then later into vinegar (acetic acid). Fermentation appears to be as old as humanity, or even older, since scientists have often observed animals in the wild enjoying fermented fruit and nectar, and it's easy to presume that prehuman primates were enjoying fermentation long before our human ancestors came along.

Vinegar is inevitable. Leave a container of wine or beer out long enough, and bacteria in the liquid (or on the container or in the surrounding air) will metabolize ethanol and oxygen into acetic acid. In fact, the process is so predictable that wine and beer makers need to take steps to halt it so as to avoid ruining their products.

Many types of vinegar are appropriate for shrub-making. The only vinegar I nearly never use, in fact, is distilled white vinegar, which lacks the savory and aromatic qualities of other vinegars. The following are the most versatile vinegars for shrub-making:

APPLE CIDER VINEGAR (ACV): The backbone of my shrubs. ACV is easy to find, inexpensive, and neutral enough in flavor to enhance many different fruits and vegetables without overpowering them. Although the flavor is neutral, it is not bland; it's tangy and reminiscent of fresh apples. Many ACVs on the market have a "mother," a cloudy layer at the bottom of the bottle. This just means the vinegar hasn't been filtered to remove by-products of fermentation. These are harmless, but you can find filtered ACV if you don't like the look of the "mother."

RED WINE VINEGAR has a character to it that reminds me of jams made from grapes and berries. It works well with big-character fruits, such as berries and cherries.

WHITE WINE & CHAMPAGNE VINEGAR have a bit of the same jammy quality, but they're sharper and brighter than red wine vinegar. This means they're better for more delicate ingredients, such as stone fruits.

Balsamic vinegar is dark and rich. I don't use it often because it can be overpowering. However, in this book I've used it in recipes starring coffee and cocoa, which are strong enough flavors to stand up to the balsamic.

Rice wine vinegar can work really well in shrubs. It's less acidic than most grape wine vinegars, and it pairs well with vegetal shrubs, such as those made with ginger, cucumber, or carrot.

One additional tip: Try blending vinegars in your shrubs. The "white" vinegars (white wine, Champagne, rice) can balance the bite of more assertive vinegars, such as ACV or red wine or balsamic.

✳ A NOTE ON FRUIT VINEGARS

When shopping for fruit vinegars, most of what you'll find on the market is fruit-*flavored* vinegar. That is a vinegar—often white wine—that has had fruit flavoring added to it, whether that's raspberry, strawberry, passion fruit, or what have you. Some vendors, however, also sell vinegar that's actually fermented from the fruit itself. In the same way that wine-based vinegars are fermented from grape wine, these vinegars are fermented from wine- or beerlike liquids made from the actual fruit. Pineapple and coconut are good examples of this.

These vinegars are available to purchase, but usually only from online specialty retailers, and they can be quite expensive. Because of the trouble and expense in obtaining them, I don't have any recipes in this book that require these ingredients. If you're adventurous, though, you might enjoy experimenting with making shrubs from them.

SHRUBS

Apple *and* Horseradish Shrub

The sharp, pungent flavor of horseradish arises from the same chemical compound that flavors mustard and wasabi. Horseradish and apple might seem like a surprising or unusual pairing, but the sweet, brisk flavor of apple marries well with the sharp pop of horseradish, softening its tang. Although you can use fresh horseradish for this, shredding it as you would the apples, prepared horseradish is easier to find, usually in a refrigerator case with other condiments. Ordinarily, the only ingredients are the bitter root itself, sugar, distilled vinegar, and a bit of salt.

3 medium apples, quartered (no need to peel, core, or seed)

2 inches horseradish, or 3 tablespoons jarred pure horseradish

1 cup apple cider vinegar

½ cup turbinado sugar

1. Using a box grater or food processor, shred the apples. If you're using a box grater, shred over a rimmed plate to retain the juices.

2. If using fresh horseradish, also shred that with the box grater or food processor.

3. Combine the shredded apples, horseradish, cider vinegar, and turbinado sugar in a nonreactive container. Cover and leave in the refrigerator for up to 2 days.

4. Place a fine-mesh strainer over a small bowl. Strain the apple mixture. Squeeze or press the mixture to remove any remaining liquid.

5. Pour the liquid into a clean mason jar or glass bottle. Add a lid or cap, then shake well to combine. Place in the refrigerator.

6. The shrub will keep for 1 year in the refrigerator.

Apple, Thyme, *and* Allspice Shrub

Apples and thyme are a classic culinary pairing, and you can find them wedded in main dishes, desserts, and beverages. The peppery sweetness of thyme deliciously complements the crisp tartness of apple, while allspice—with its notes of clove, cinnamon, and nutmeg—rounds out the flavor with earthy appeal. If you'd like to riff on this recipe with your own pairings, apples also play well with such herbs as mint, rosemary, sage, and tarragon, and such spices as black pepper, cardamom, cloves, coriander, nutmeg, and star anise.

3 medium apples, quartered (no need to peel, core, or seed)

1 cup apple cider vinegar

½ cup granulated sugar

1 tablespoon fresh thyme leaves

½ teaspoon ground allspice

1. Using a box grater or food processor, shred the apples. If you're using a box grater, shred over a rimmed plate to retain the juices.

2. Combine the shredded apples, cider vinegar, sugar, thyme, and allspice in a nonreactive container. Cover and leave in the refrigerator for up to 2 days.

3. Place a fine-mesh strainer over a small bowl. Strain the apple mixture. Squeeze or press the mixture to remove any remaining liquid.

4. Pour the liquid into a clean mason jar or glass bottle. Add a lid or cap, then shake well to combine. Place in the refrigerator.

5. The shrub will keep for 1 year in the refrigerator.

Apricot, Basil, *and* Balsamic Shrub

Summer means different things to different people, but for me it's the season of plump stone fruit, juicy berries, and rich tomatoes. Apricots and basil combine for a flavor that is sweet, tangy, and earthy. I use balsamic here to round out that earthiness with a rich fragrant tartness. Because the apricot is a botanical relative of the plum and the plum-apricot hybrid known as the pluot, either fruit can swap in this shrub in place of the apricot.

- 1 pound apricots, pitted and sliced (but leave the skins on)
- 1 cup granulated sugar
- 15 to 20 fresh basil leaves (about ½ ounce), bruised
- 1 cup balsamic vinegar

1. Place the apricots and sugar in a medium bowl. Mash up the apricots and stir to combine.
2. Add the basil and balsamic vinegar. Stir again to combine.
3. Cover the bowl with plastic wrap and place in the refrigerator. Allow to macerate for up to 2 days.
4. Position a fine-mesh strainer over a small bowl and pour the apricot mixture through it to remove the solids.
5. Pour into a clean mason jar. Cap the jar, shake well to incorporate any undissolved sugar, and leave in the refrigerator for a week before using.
6. The shrub will keep for 1 year in the refrigerator.

Basil Shrub

I've noticed in recent years that bartenders have been making simple shrubs based on single herbs, or two or more herbs in combination. These bartenders seem to be using these shrubs as they might a tincture (a solution of an herb or two in alcohol). Tinctures are used to provide a small amount of concentrated herbal flavor, measured into cocktails in drops or dashes. A simple herbal shrub as this would taste great with gin—whether stirred into a gin and tonic, or mixed into a martini. I have two more herbal shrub recipes in the book, but feel free to experiment with others as well. Any leafy herb should work in this preparation, such as parsley, cilantro, thyme, chives, dill, or oregano.

30 to 40 fresh basil leaves (about 1 ounce), bruised

1 cup white wine vinegar

1 cup granulated sugar

1. Place the basil leaves in a nonreactive container, cover with the white wine vinegar, and leave in the refrigerator for up to 2 days.

2. Strain off the basil leaves, reserving the liquid. Discard the leaves. Bottle or jar the liquid. Add the sugar, add a lid or cap, then shake well to combine. Leave in the fridge for 1 week before using.

3. The shrub will keep for 1 year in the refrigerator.

NOTE: To bruise herbs, place the leaves in the palm of your hand. With your other hand, sharply slap the leaves. This releases essential oils trapped in the cells of the herb.

Banana *and* Coconut Shrub *with* Cinnamon *and* Clove

Banana and coconut are commonly paired in baked goods, such as muffins, fritters, or quick breads, or in desserts. I thought they'd work well together in a shrub as well, especially with warm spices such as cinnamon and cloves. I mentioned elsewhere that banana and pineapple vinegars are available at some specialty retailers. It's also possible to find vinegar made from fermented coconut, but again these types of specialty vinegars aren't always easy to find, and they can be expensive.

1 very ripe banana (yellow with some black spots), peeled and cut into 1-inch pieces

½ cup dried unsweetened coconut

1 cinnamon stick

5 whole cloves

¾ cup turbinado sugar

1 cup white wine vinegar

1. Place the banana pieces in a heatproof bowl, along with the coconut, cinnamon stick, and cloves.
2. Combine the turbinado sugar and white wine vinegar in a small saucepan over medium heat. Stir until the sugar dissolves.
3. Pour the vinegar mixture over the banana, coconut, cinnamon stick, and cloves. Cover and leave in the refrigerator for up to 2 days.
4. Place a fine-mesh strainer over a small bowl. Strain the banana mixture. Squeeze or press the mixture to remove any remaining liquid.
5. Pour the liquid into a clean mason jar or glass bottle. Add a lid or cap, then shake well to combine. Place in the refrigerator.
6. The shrub will keep for 1 year in the refrigerator.

Banana *and* Pineapple Shrub *with* Nutmeg

For my first book on shrubs, I never quite got around to using banana as a main ingredient, and I always regretted that, and so I'm making it up to myself here. Anyone who likes piña coladas (and getting caught in the rain) already knows these ingredients partner well. For the pineapple, you can certainly buy a whole pineapple and cut it up yourself, but if you can get precut fresh pineapple from the produce section of your grocery store, that will be fine, too. Just don't use canned pineapple, especially sweetened.

1 very ripe banana (yellow with some black spots), peeled and cut into 1-inch pieces

½ cup cubed pineapple

2 teaspoons grated nutmeg

¾ cup turbinado sugar

1 cup white wine vinegar

1. Place the banana, pineapple, and nutmeg in a heatproof bowl.
2. Combine the turbinado sugar and white wine vinegar in a small saucepan over medium heat. Stir until the sugar dissolves.
3. Pour the vinegar mixture over the banana, pineapple, and nutmeg. Cover and leave in the refrigerator for up to 2 days.
4. Place a fine-mesh strainer over a small bowl. Strain the banana mixture. Squeeze or press the mixture to remove any remaining liquid.
5. Pour the liquid into a clean mason jar or glass bottle. Add a lid or cap, then shake well to combine. Place in the refrigerator.
6. The shrub will keep for 1 year in the refrigerator.

Blood Orange, Ginger, *and* Old Bay Shrub

I love blood oranges—how they look, how they taste. I remember the first time I took one to work in my lunchbox, and when I peeled it, a coworker was shocked by the color. This shrub mixes the raspberry-hued richness of blood orange with ginger—always a good match for citrus—and Old Bay, a seafood seasoning mix from Maryland that mixes celery seed, paprika, cardamom, and other spices. Since Old Bay has a hint of ginger, it certainly complements the ginger in this shrub and lends depth to the blood orange base.

4 blood oranges

¾ cup turbinado sugar

¾ cup Champagne vinegar

2 tablespoons grated ginger

1 teaspoon Old Bay Seasoning

1. Zest the blood oranges and then build an oleo-saccharum using the turbinado sugar and zest, as described on page 94. Allow to rest on the countertop overnight.

2. Meanwhile, pour the Champagne vinegar over the grated ginger in a medium bowl. Juice the oranges and add the juice to the bowl of vinegar. Stir to combine. Leave in the refrigerator overnight.

3. Place a fine-mesh strainer over a separate medium bowl. Pour the vinegar mixture through the strainer. Press or squeeze to extract all the liquid.

4. Add the oleo-saccharum and Old Bay. Stir to combine. Transfer to a jar or bottle, seal, and shake to further blend the ingredients. Allow 2 to 3 days for the flavors to meld.

5. The shrub will keep for 1 year in the refrigerator.

Blueberry, Cinnamon, *and* Clove Shrub

Cinnamon brings to a dish—or a shrub—a flavor that is warm and woody, with a touch of spicy heat. Cloves have a bitter astringency coupled with a sweet pungent aroma. Together, they bring intensity to blueberries. Try this on ice cream or blended with yogurt into a smoothie.

1 pint blueberries

1 cup granulated sugar

1 cinnamon stick

5 cloves

1 cup apple cider vinegar

1. Place the blueberries and sugar in a medium bowl. Crush the berries and stir to combine.

2. Add the cinnamon stick, cloves, and cider vinegar. Stir again to combine.

3. Cover the bowl with plastic wrap and place in the refrigerator. Allow to macerate up to 2 days.

4. Position a fine-mesh strainer over a small bowl and pour the blueberry mixture through it to remove the solids.

5. Pour into a clean mason jar. Cap, shake well to incorporate any undissolved sugar, and leave in the refrigerator for a week before using.

6. The shrub will keep for 1 year in the refrigerator.

Blackberry *and* Black Pepper Shrub

A little black magic in this one... juicy berries and spicy peppercorns mix to bring a summery shrub with a bit of zing. The piney and citrusy notes of black peppercorn bring complexity and not just heat to the tart, earthy succulence of summer blackberries.

1½ cups blackberries, mashed lightly

¾ cup granulated sugar

1 tablespoon coarsely ground black pepper

¾ cup apple cider vinegar

1. Place all the ingredients in a medium bowl. Stir to combine. Cover with plastic wrap and place in the refrigerator. Allow to macerate for up to 2 days.

2. Place a fine-mesh strainer over a small bowl and pour the mixture through it to remove the solids.

3. Pour the vinegar mixture into a clean mason jar. Cap, shake well to incorporate any undissolved sugar, and leave in the refrigerator for a week before using.

4. The shrub will keep for 1 year in the refrigerator.

Cantaloupe, Fennel, *and* Star Anise Shrub

Cantaloupe has a delicate and flavor that pairs well with the licorice qualities of fennel and star anise. Because of its delicacy, I chose a light vinegar to pair with it. If you can't find Champagne vinegar, white wine vinegar will work as well. Cantaloupe is often available precut in the produce section, and if you can find it that way, it's a great convenience.

- 1 cup peeled, cubed, and seeded cantaloupe
- ½ cup chopped fennel bulb, stalks and fronds saved for another use
- ¾ cup granulated sugar
- 4 star anise pods
- ¾ cup Champagne vinegar

1. Place all the ingredients in a medium bowl. Stir to combine. Cover with plastic wrap and place in the refrigerator. Allow to macerate for up to 2 days.
2. Position a fine-mesh strainer over a small bowl and pour the mixture through it to remove the solids.
3. Pour the mixture into a clean mason jar. Cap, shake well to incorporate any undissolved sugar, and leave in the refrigerator for a week before using.
4. The shrub will keep for 1 year in the refrigerator.

Chamomile, Pear, *and* Lavender Shrub

Chamomile, the word, arises from Greek words meaning "earth apple," and sure enough, chamomile, the tea, carries hints of apple with a mellow sweetness. The applelike quality of the tea gives it a natural affinity for pears. Lavender, a member of the mint family, has a long history as a culinary herb. With a flavor somewhat like (though mellower than) mint and rosemary, it also pairs well with pears.

3 large pears, quartered (no need to peel, core, or seed)

½ cup apple cider vinegar

½ cup granulated sugar

3 tablespoons (or 3 tea bags) dried chamomile

1 tablespoon dried lavender

½ cup boiling water

1. Using a box grater or a food processor, shred the pears.
2. Combine the shredded pears, cider vinegar, and sugar in a nonreactive container. Cover and leave in a cool place on the countertop for up to 2 days.
3. After 2 days, place a fine-mesh strainer over a small bowl. Strain away the pear solids. Squeeze or press the mixture to remove any remaining liquid.
4. Place the chamomile and lavender in a jar or mug and pour in the boiling water. Let the tea steep for 10 minutes, and then pour through a fine-mesh sieve, pressing on the solids with a spoon to extract all the concentrated flavor. Discard the solids and let the tea cool completely.
5. Add the tea to the pear syrup and stir to combine well.
6. The shrub will keep for 1 year in the refrigerator.

Carrot *and* Fenugreek Shrub

I love savory shrubs. I find that vegetables make shrubs taste earthy and rich, without too much sweetness. Here, the bright, crisp flavor of the carrots melds well with fenugreek seeds, a spice commonly used in Indian and Middle Eastern cuisines. Fenugreek carries a hint of maple, providing a flavor of maple-glazed carrots to this shrub. Tangentially, starting in around 2005, an aroma of maple syrup began wafting over the island of Manhattan from time to time. The culprit, it turns out, was a facility in New Jersey that processed fenugreek.

2 pounds carrots

¾ cup white wine vinegar

¼ cup turbinado sugar

1 tablespoon fenugreek seeds, crushed lightly

1. Wash the carrots and, if necessary, scrub with a vegetable brush to remove any dirt. Peel them if you wish, but it's not necessary.

2. Puree the carrots in a blender or food processor.

3. Pour the carrot puree into a nonreactive container.

4. Add the white wine vinegar, turbinado sugar, and fenugreek seeds. Stir to combine. Cover and refrigerate for 2 days.

5. Place a fine-mesh strainer over a small bowl. Strain the carrot mixture. Press or squeeze the mixture to remove any remaining liquid.

6. Pour the liquid into a clean mason jar or glass bottle. Add a lid or cap, then shake well to combine. Place in the refrigerator.

7. The shrub will keep for 1 year in the refrigerator.

Carrot, Apple, *and* Caraway Shrub

This shrub entices you with the scent of caraway, reminiscent of rye bread. The carrot is the main flavor on the sip, though, with the apple mildly sweetening the flavor and amplifying the carrot. A cousin of fennel, caraway carries a hint of licorice and citrus in its aroma. Caraway is also a flavoring ingredient in the Scandinavian liquor aquavit, and in fact, this shrub would be fantastic with aquavit. If you can't find aquavit, try gin.

1½ pounds carrots

2 medium apples, quartered (no need to peel, core, or seed)

1 cup apple cider vinegar

½ cup granulated sugar

1 tablespoon caraway seeds, crushed lightly

1. Wash the carrots and, if necessary, scrub with a vegetable brush to remove any dirt. Peel them if you wish, but it's not necessary.
2. Puree the carrots and apples in a blender or food processor.
3. Pour the puree into a nonreactive container.
4. Add the cider vinegar, sugar, and caraway seeds. Stir to combine. Cover and refrigerate for 2 days.
5. Place a fine-mesh strainer over a small bowl. Strain the carrot mixture. Press or squeeze the mixture to remove any remaining liquid.
6. Pour the liquid into a clean mason jar or glass bottle. Add a lid or cap, then shake well to combine. Place in the refrigerator.
7. The shrub will keep for 1 year in the refrigerator.

Cilantro, Lime, *and* Jalapeño Shrub

> Sometimes you come up with a shrub idea so obvious, you wonder why it took you so long to think of it. This is one of those—cilantro, lime, and jalapeño are just made for one another. The cilantro is lemony and grassy, peppery and pungent. These qualities mesh well with the citrus tang of lime and the gentle, fruity heat of jalapeño. If cilantro tastes like soap to you, though, perhaps take a pass on this one. I, however, think it's lovely.

- 6 medium limes
- ¾ cup turbinado sugar
- 1 small jalapeño pepper, stemmed, seeded, and diced finely
- ½ cup fresh cilantro (leaves and tender stems)
- ¾ cup Champagne vinegar

1. Zest the limes and then build an oleo-saccharum using the turbinado sugar and zest, as described on page 94. Allow to rest on the countertop overnight.

2. Meanwhile, place the jalapeño and cilantro in a medium bowl and pour the Champagne vinegar over them. Juice the limes and add the juice to the bowl. Stir to combine. Refrigerate overnight.

3. Place a fine-mesh strainer over a separate medium bowl. Pour the vinegar mixture into the strainer. Press or squeeze to extract all the vinegar.

4. Add the oleo-saccharum. Stir to combine. Transfer to a jar or bottle, seal, and shake to further blend the ingredients. Allow 2 to 3 days for flavors to meld before using.

5. The shrub will keep for 1 year in the refrigerator.

Coconut *and* Lemongrass Shrub

Sometimes, when you think about getting into the kitchen, the normal things you cook just seem to bore you, and you want to try new things instead. Such was my feeling when I was creating recipes for this book; I wanted to branch out into new shrub ingredients. Coconuts are mildly sweet, nutty, and somewhat woody. Lemongrass, despite its name, is no relative of citrus fruits, but rather an actual grass that just happens to taste similar to lemons, with also a hint of ginger. Of course, lemongrass and coconut are staples in Southeast Asian cuisine, so I knew they'd work together here.

2 fresh lemongrass stalks

½ cup dried unsweetened coconut

2 cups white wine vinegar

½ cup turbinado sugar

1 cup water

1. Peel away the outer layers of the lemongrass. Remove the root end and about 6 inches from the top leafy end where the green meets the white, leaving 3 to 4 inches of the white middle. Smash the lemongrass with a flat object, to release its essential oils. Cut the lemongrass into rings and place in a jar with a lid.

2. Add the coconut, white wine vinegar, turbinado sugar, and water. Shake well and steep in the refrigerator for at least 1 day, and up to 2 weeks for a more potent flavor.

3. Place a fine-mesh strainer over a medium bowl. Pour the mixture into the strainer. Press or squeeze to extract all the vinegar.

4. The shrub will keep for 1 year in the refrigerator.

Cherry *and* Cocoa Shrub *with* Cinnamon

This rich, not-too-sweet shrub exudes fragrances of dark chocolate and sweet-sour cherry, reminiscent of a Black Forest cake. The balsamic, rather than overpowering the other ingredients, makes them even richer and more intense. This would be delicious blended with soda as a grown-up soft drink, mixed with rum or bourbon in a cocktail, or spooned over ice cream.

- 2 cups sweet cherries, stemmed and pitted
- ½ cup balsamic vinegar
- ¼ teaspoon ground cinnamon
- ½ teaspoon vanilla extract
- 2 tablespoons unsweetened dark cocoa powder
- ¼ cup granulated sugar

1. Combine all the ingredients in a saucepan, bring to a boil, lower the heat, and simmer for 30 minutes, stirring a few times. Remove from the heat and let cool.

2. Strain once or twice through a fine-mesh strainer into a small bowl, until the mixture is clear and smooth looking.

3. Funnel into a glass container with a spout or a mason jar.

4. The shrub will keep for 1 year in the refrigerator.

Coffee Shrub *with* Raspberry *and* Thyme

As the title implies, this recipe yields a coffee shrub with notes of raspberry and thyme, not a raspberry shrub with hints of coffee. This is an important distinction; the shrub tastes more like flavored coffee than it does like raspberries. I made mine with coffee that I ground at home just before testing the recipe, but purchasing ground coffee should work, as long as it's fresh. The funny thing about this is, I normally dislike flavored coffee, especially the fruity stuff. But I think that's because the fruit flavor is usually artificial, and tastes of it. This, however, is delicious.

1 cup coarsely ground coffee

8 sprigs thyme

¼ cup water

1 cup balsamic vinegar

2 cups raspberries

1 cup granulated sugar

1. Combine the ground coffee, thyme, water, and vinegar in a medium bowl, cover with plastic wrap, and let sit overnight.

2. Place the raspberries and sugar in a separate medium bowl. Crush the berries, then stir to combine. Cover with plastic wrap and macerate in the refrigerator for up to 2 days.

3. Position a fine-mesh strainer, lined with cheesecloth or a coffee filter, over a small bowl and pour the coffee mixture through it to remove the fine grit from the coffee.

4. Position a second mesh strainer over another bowl and pour the raspberry mixture through it to remove any solids.

5. Combine with the coffee mixture in a clean mason jar. Cap, shake well to incorporate any undissolved sugar, and leave in the refrigerator for a week before using.

6. The shrub will keep for 1 year in the refrigerator.

Cranberry *and* Pine Needle Shrub

This recipe is another example of my wanting to stretch my wings a bit and try something unusual. Consider this a great shrub for fall and winter entertaining. However, just because I wanted to try something novel doesn't mean I wanted to take a risk on my ingredients. I've never foraged for loose pine needles that you might find in a wooded area in the fall. Not all of them are safe to use, and I don't want to make any dumb mistakes. To be safe, I strongly suggest using a commercial pine needle tea, which you can find on Amazon and in some health-food stores. Commercially sold teas, in the United States anyway, are made from the needles of the eastern white pine, which are a great source of vitamin C.

1 cup cranberries (frozen cranberries, thawed before using, are just fine)

¾ cup apple cider vinegar

¾ cup turbinado sugar

2 tea bags pine needle tea, or 2 tablespoons loose pine needle tea

1. Combine the cranberries, cider vinegar, and turbinado sugar in a blender. Blend until pureed.

2. Transfer to a nonreactive container. Cover and leave in a cool place for up to 2 days.

3. After 2 days, place a fine-mesh strainer over a small bowl. Strain the cranberry mixture. Squeeze or press to remove any remaining liquid.

4. Meanwhile, prepare the tea according to the package instructions. When cool, add to the cranberry mixture.

5. Pour into a jar or bottle, add a lid or cap, and shake well to combine.

6. The shrub will keep for 1 year in the refrigerator.

Cucumber, Cilantro, *and* Coriander Shrub

A cooling shrub perfect for summer, this recipe pairs cucumber and cilantro for a light refresher. Because of the delicacy of cucumber's flavor, I call for a light rice vinegar here, though white wine vinegar will work just as well. To back up the cilantro, I bring in a bit of its seed—ground coriander. I include the salt just to make the flavor a bit more savory; the shrub won't taste salty.

- 2 large cucumbers (peeled if desired, but that's not necessary)
- 1 cup rice wine vinegar
- ½ cup granulated sugar
- 1 teaspoon kosher salt
- ½ cup fresh cilantro, chopped
- 1 tablespoon ground coriander

1. Place the cucumbers in a blender. Blend until pureed.
2. Press the puree through a fine-mesh strainer into a medium bowl.
3. Combine the cucumber juice and remaining ingredients in a jar or bottle. Shake well, then steep in the refrigerator for 2 days.
4. Strain through a fine-mesh strainer into a medium bowl, discard the solids, then return the shrub to its jar or bottle.
5. The shrub will keep for 1 year in the refrigerator.

Fennel *and* Tarragon Shrub

One for the licorice lovers! Fennel and tarragon both contain estragole, a chemical that contributes an anise flavor. If you like absinthe or pastis, you'll enjoy this as well. (And in fact, fennel is an ingredient in absinthe.) Other herbs that contain estragole include anise, bay, and basil, so feel free to swap any of those in if you can't find tarragon.

1 fennel bulb, chopped, stalks and fronds saved for another use

1 cup granulated sugar

2 sprigs fresh tarragon

1 cup apple cider vinegar

1. Place all the ingredients in a medium bowl. Stir to combine. Cover with plastic wrap and place in the refrigerator. Allow to macerate for up to 2 days.

2. After 2 days, squeeze the fennel with clean hands.

3. Place a fine-mesh strainer over a small bowl and pour the mixture through it to remove the solids.

4. Pour into a clean mason jar. Cap, shake well to incorporate any undissolved sugar, and leave in the refrigerator for 1 week before using.

5. The shrub will keep for 1 year in the refrigerator.

Fig, Clove, *and* Vanilla Shrub

Cloves carry a flavor that is sweet but a little musty and reminiscent of gingerbread. The flavor comes from the compound eugenol, also found in vanilla, which makes these flavors combine well in this shrub. Together, the clove and vanilla round out and enrich the flavor and aroma of figs.

2 cups chopped fresh figs

½ cup balsamic vinegar

½ cup water

½ teaspoon vanilla extract

½ teaspoon ground clove

1 teaspoon freshly squeezed lemon juice

½ cup turbinado sugar

1. Combine all the ingredients in a saucepan, then bring to a boil, lower the heat, and simmer for 30 minutes, stirring a few times. Remove from the heat and let cool.

2. Place a fine-mesh strainer over a small bowl and strain once or twice, until the mixture is clear and smooth looking.

3. Funnel into a glass container with a spout, or a mason jar.

4. The shrub will keep for 1 year in the refrigerator.

Fig *and* Green Anise Shrub

Figs! Man, I love figs. Like many American kids, I "met" figs through the fruit-and-cake afterschool treat, the Fig Newton. I find the rich, berrylike flavor of figs really appealing, and here I pair figs with licorice-like anise. The anise nicely complements the nutty spice of figs. This shrub uses a slightly different process than others in this book. I've never been able to simply macerate figs in sugar to remove their juice, the way I do, say, peaches or strawberries. In this recipe, I infuse figgy flavor into vinegar by steeping them together for a couple of days. In the next recipe, I use the hot process to get figgy flavor into the shrub. Either method works; it's just that the cold process tastes more like fresh figs and the hot process like cooked figs.

1 pint purple figs, pureed in a blender

1 cup apple cider vinegar

1 teaspoon green aniseeds

1 cup turbinado sugar

1. Place the pureed figs, cider vinegar, and aniseeds in a medium bowl. Stir to combine. Cover with plastic wrap and place in the refrigerator. Allow to macerate for up to 2 days.

2. Strain out the fig solids and aniseeds. Pour the liquid into a bottle or jar, add the turbinado sugar, and shake. Allow to sit in the refrigerator for at least a week before using.

3. The shrub will keep for 1 year in the refrigerator.

Fire Cider Shrub

Fire cider has a long reputation as a health tonic, thought to aid with relieving colds and sniffles, unclogging sinuses, boosting immunity, and improving digestion. Although variations on this recipe have been around for centuries, the name arose in the 1970s from the kitchen of an American herbalist named Rosemary Gladstar. However, no medical evidence exists to show that it works. But that's fine; many people drink it just because they enjoy the taste! This might not be a cure-all, but a tasty beverage is its own reward. However, do take note of the name! Fire cider is . . . well . . . fiery, with horseradish, ginger, turmeric, and peppercorns bringing the heat.

- ½ cup coarsely chopped horseradish (no need to peel)
- 8 large cloves garlic, chopped coarsely
- 1 small onion, chopped coarsely
- ¼ cup coarsely chopped fresh ginger (no need to peel)
- 1 lemon, quartered and sliced thinly (leave the peel on!)
- 4 sprigs rosemary
- 1 tablespoon ground turmeric, or 2 tablespoons grated fresh organic turmeric
- 1 teaspoon black peppercorns
- 2 to 3 cups raw unfiltered apple cider vinegar
- ¼ cup raw honey, or more to taste

continues

1. Place the horseradish, garlic, onion, ginger, lemon slices, rosemary, turmeric, and peppercorns in a quart-size glass jar. Cover with enough cider vinegar to cover. Cap tightly and shake to combine.

2. Let the jar sit in the refrigerator for 1 month.

3. Place a fine-mesh strainer over a small bowl. Strain the mixture. Squeeze or press the mixture to remove any remaining liquid.

4. Clean your jar and lid, then pour the strained liquid back in. Add the honey, cap, and shake to combine. Taste and add more honey if needed.

5. The shrub will keep for 1 year in the refrigerator.

NOTE: This needs to steep for at least a month in your kitchen. You'll need a 1-quart jar with a plastic lid.

Green Tea *and* Ginger Shrub

This delicate and yet spicy shrub takes its base from green tea, which has grassy, flowery, earthy, and vegetal flavors. It's made from the same leaves as black tea, but green tea undergoes less oxidation, thus producing a milder flavor. The grassy earthiness meshes well with ginger's kicky, spicy flavor, and the cinnamon provides sweetness and a hint of warmth. These ingredients combine for a well-balanced shrub with depth and a lot of character.

2 tablespoons grated fresh ginger

1 cup apple cider vinegar

2 cups water

8 tea bags green tea

1 cup granulated sugar

1 cinnamon stick

1. Place the grated ginger in a nonreactive container. Pour the cider vinegar over the ginger. Stir to combine. Leave in a cool, dark place for 2 days.

2. Place a fine-mesh strainer over a medium bowl. Pour the vinegar mixture through the strainer. Press or squeeze, to extract all the vinegar.

3. Combine the water, green tea, sugar, and cinnamon stick in a medium saucepan over medium heat. Bring to a boil. Lower the heat and simmer for 5 minutes. Remove from the heat. Remove and discard the cinnamon stick.

4. Mix together the tea syrup and ginger-flavored vinegar in a jar and seal tightly.

5. The shrub will keep for 1 year in the refrigerator.

Grape *and* Rosemary Shrub

Rosemary is an earthy and woody herb, similar to thyme or oregano, and with flavor hints of pepper and lemon. In this shrub, I paired rosemary with juicy sweet grapes. Any table grape from the supermarket will do well here. The mild, sweet floral notes of grapes pair well with any earthy herb, such as rosemary, thyme, or oregano, so feel free to switch things up, or even try combining two herbs in this shrub.

1 pound grapes, mashed lightly

½ cup granulated sugar

5 sprigs rosemary

½ cup sherry vinegar

1. Place all the ingredients in a medium bowl. Stir to combine. Cover with plastic wrap and place in the refrigerator. Allow to macerate for up to 2 days.

2. Position a fine-mesh strainer over a small bowl and pour the grape mixture through it to remove the solids.

3. Pour into a clean mason jar. Cap, shake well to incorporate any undissolved sugar, and leave in the refrigerator for a week before using.

4. The shrub will keep for 1 year in the refrigerator.

Habanero, Watermelon, *and* Thyme Shrub

Hot! Cool! This shrub weds spicy habanero with thirst-quenching watermelon for a combination that zaps the palate while also being refreshing. You can sometimes find cubed watermelon for sale in the produce section, if you don't want to do the work yourself; it'll be just as good as cutting up whole watermelon.

2 to 3 habanero peppers, stemmed, seeded, and diced

1½ cups cubed, seeded watermelon

¾ cup granulated sugar

¾ cup white wine vinegar

1. Place the peppers, watermelon, and sugar in a medium bowl. Stir to combine. Cover with plastic wrap and place in the refrigerator. Allow to macerate for up to 2 days.

2. Position a fine-mesh strainer over a small bowl and pour the mixture through it to remove the solids.

3. Combine the strained syrup with the white wine vinegar. Whisk well to incorporate any undissolved sugar.

4. Pour the mixture into a clean mason jar. Cap, shake well to incorporate any undissolved sugar, and leave in the refrigerator for a week before using.

5. The shrub will keep for 1 year in the refrigerator.

Hibiscus Shrub

Hibiscus is a type of flowering plant that grows in warmer regions of the world. Tangy and subtly sweet, with mild notes of citrus, hibiscus is quite versatile and pairs well with a number of different flavors, such as ginger, cloves, cardamom, cinnamon, honey, dates, pineapple, berries, and melon. Creating your own flavors—raspberry hibiscus, for example, or pineapple cardamom hibiscus—should be easy and rewarding. If you can't find dried hibiscus, you might be able to find hibiscus tea in the coffee and tea aisle. I used brown sugar here because I like how its richness works with the floral aromas of hibiscus.

1 cup dried hibiscus flowers

¾ cup dark brown sugar

1 cinnamon stick

One 1-inch piece of ginger, sliced thinly

1 cup water

¾ cup apple cider vinegar

1. Combine the hibiscus flowers, brown sugar, cinnamon stick, sliced ginger, and water in a medium saucepan over medium-high heat. Bring to a boil, lower the heat, and simmer until the sugar dissolves.

2. Remove from the heat and stir in the cider vinegar. Stir until combined.

3. Strain through a fine-mesh strainer into a medium bowl. Discard the solids. Let cool to room temperature, then bottle and store in the fridge.

4. The shrub will keep for 1 year in the refrigerator.

Honeydew, Fig, *and* Mint Shrub

Honeydew is a refreshing fruit. I wish I enjoyed it, but for some reason I've never taken to melons of any kind. I understand why people enjoy it on a hot day, though: it's 90 percent water. As an excellent source of vitamin C, it's also a great fruit to have around. Though I might not like the melon on its own, I love it in this shrub, where it joins with earthy figs and bright, peppery mint for a tart summer quencher. Again, you might be able to find it precut in your produce section, and that's a fine shortcut to take.

1 cup cubed and seeded honeydew melon

1 pint purple figs

1 cup turbinado sugar

15 to 20 fresh mint leaves (about ½ ounce), bruised

1 cup apple cider vinegar

1. Combine the honeydew, figs, and turbinado sugar in a blender, and blend until pureed.

2. Pour into a medium bowl and add the mint and cider vinegar. Stir to combine. Cover with plastic wrap and place in the refrigerator. Allow to macerate for up to 2 days.

3. Position a fine-mesh strainer over a small bowl and pour the honeydew mixture through it to remove any solids.

4. Pour the mixture into a clean mason jar. Cap, shake well to incorporate any undissolved sugar, and leave in the refrigerator for a week before using.

5. The shrub will keep for 1 year in the refrigerator.

Lavender Shrub

These herbal shrubs (this one, the Basil Shrub [page 48], and the Rosemary and Sage Shrub [page 112]) are so easy to make, and yet so nicely flavorful. Lavender is splendidly aromatic, floral, and lemony, with a mildly sweet flavor reminiscent of spring. This shrub is great in soda water as a beverage and also blended with gin or vodka, but I also really enjoy it as a component in salad dressings.

3 tablespoons culinary-grade dried lavender

1 cup white wine vinegar

1 cup granulated sugar

1. Place the lavender in a nonreactive container, cover with the white wine vinegar, and store in a cool, dark place for 1 day.

2. Strain off the lavender, reserving the liquid. Discard the leaves. Bottle or jar the liquid. Add the sugar, lid it up, and shake well to combine. Leave in the fridge for 1 week.

3. The shrub will keep for 1 year in the refrigerator.

NOTE: Lavender is an herb with a deep history in food, cosmetics, and medicine. The term lavender describes dozens of species of flower in the genus *Lavandula*. Some species are better used in soaps and lotions than in food or beverages, however. Culinary-grade lavender is sweeter and less oily than that used in cosmetics. For shrub-making, look for dried lavender in the spice aisle of your grocery store.

Mango *and* Basil Shrub

Mango is a mildly sweet fruit, with a flavor that tastes like a cross between peach and pineapple. Basil might seem an unlikely pairing, but the flavors do interact well with each other. What basil brings to mango is a pungent grassiness, married with a hint of spice, which complements the sweet peachiness of mango. This shrub would pair well with either tequila or gin and any form of citrus in cocktails. Mango's light flavor, to me, seemed to call for a light vinegar, such as Champagne vinegar.

1½ cups peeled, pitted, and cubed fresh mango

1 cup granulated sugar

15 to 20 fresh basil leaves (about ½ ounce), bruised

1 cup Champagne vinegar

1. Place all the ingredients in a medium bowl. Stir to combine. Cover with plastic wrap and place in the refrigerator. Allow to macerate for up to 2 days.

2. Position a fine-mesh strainer over a small bowl and pour the mixture through it to remove the solids.

3. Pour the mixture into a clean mason jar. Cap, shake well to incorporate any undissolved sugar, and place in the refrigerator for a week before using.

4. The shrub will keep for 1 year in the refrigerator.

Mango *and* Passion Fruit Shrub *with* Black Pepper *and* Mint

Mango is a stone fruit originating in South and Southeast Asia, with flavors of peach and pineapple. Passion fruit, on the other hand, hails from South America and tastes of kiwi, melon, and also pineapple. The flavor affinities of the two fruits mean they blend well together into a shrub, creating a flavor a lot like the tropical punch drinks many of us enjoyed as kids. For this shrub, I decided to zhuzh them up with peppercorns and fresh mint. You can use either Champagne vinegar or white wine vinegar in this.

½ cup peeled, pitted, and cubed fresh mango

½ cup diced fresh passion fruit

¼ cup freshly squeezed lime juice

¾ cup granulated sugar

15 to 20 fresh mint leaves (about ½ ounce), bruised

1 tablespoon whole black peppercorns

¾ cup Champagne vinegar

1. Place the mango, passion fruit, lime juice, and sugar in a medium bowl. Mash up the fruit and stir to combine. Add the mint, peppercorns, and Champagne vinegar, and stir again. Cover with plastic wrap and place in the refrigerator. Allow to macerate for up to 2 days.

2. Position a fine-mesh strainer over a small bowl and pour the fruit mixture through it to remove the solids.

3. Pour the mixture into a clean mason jar. Cap, shake well to incorporate any undissolved sugar, and leave in the refrigerator for a week before using.

4. The shrub will keep for 1 year in the refrigerator.

Meyer Lemon *and* Za'atar Shrub

Za'atar is the name of both a wild herb and a spice blend. The herb itself tastes a bit like marjoram, oregano, or thyme—or perhaps some combo of the three. To highlight this similarity, the spice blend, depending on the brand you choose, often contains oregano or thyme alongside chile peppers (in some brands) and dried za'atar leaves. Rounding out the blend are ground sumac, which contributes a tart citrus flavor, and sesame seeds, which provide nuttiness. The complexity of za'atar lends itself well to the orange hints you find in Meyer lemons. I have you start with a teaspoon of za'atar in this recipe, since different brands have distinctive flavors. You can always add more, but if the za'atar is too chile-hot for you, you can't take that back out once you've added it.

4 Meyer lemons

¾ cup turbinado sugar

¾ cup Champagne vinegar

1 teaspoon za'atar

1. Zest the Meyer lemons and then build an oleo-saccharum using the turbinado sugar and zest, as described on page 94.

2. Juice the Meyer lemons and add the juice to a bowl with the Champagne vinegar, za'atar, and oleo-saccharum. Stir to combine. Transfer to a jar or bottle, seal, and shake to further mix the ingredients. Store in the refrigerator, and allow 2 to 3 days for flavors to meld.

3. The shrub will keep for 1 year in the refrigerator.

Mint *and* Ginger Shrub

Mint is an aromatic herb, from the genus *Mentha,* found in dozens of species and hybrids. Mint grows year-round, and if you ever had it in your garden, you probably know it can take over. Commercially, the most commonly found species are spearmint and peppermint. Either will work in this recipe, although the peppermint is, well, a bit more peppery. Ginger is a flowering plant, though what we eat is its rhizome or rootstalk. Its relatives include galangal and turmeric.

½ **cup fresh mint leaves**

½ **cup grated fresh ginger**

¾ **cup apple cider vinegar**

½ **cup freshly squeezed lime juice**

½ **cup granulated sugar**

1. Place the mint leaves in a medium bowl and gently bruise with a wooden muddler or wooden spoon.

2. Place all the remaining ingredients in the same bowl. Stir to combine. Cover with plastic wrap and place in the refrigerator. Allow to macerate for up to 2 days.

3. Position a fine-mesh strainer over a small bowl and pour the grape mixture through it to remove the solids.

4. Pour into a clean mason jar. Cap, shake well to incorporate any undissolved sugar, and leave in the refrigerator for a week before using.

5. The shrub will keep for 1 year in the refrigerator.

Olive, Lemon, *and* Juniper Shrub

A few years ago, after I published my first book on shrubs, the *New York Times* ran an article about dirty martinis, which detailed a version from the now-defunct New York City bar Saxon + Parole. The S + P version of a dirty martini was, quite frankly, well out of the grasp of a home mixologist or even a booze scribe such as yours truly: it used a custom-made olive distillate, bitters made with olives from four countries, and olive shrub. I thought, *I can't make the olive distillate, and I can't make the bitters, but I can make the shrub, gosh darn it*, and that's what I've done—albeit over 10 years after I read the *Times* article. I don't have any idea whether this is anything close to the S + P version; I just know it's delicious, and it should give you the briny satisfaction you're looking for if you love dirty martinis.

1½ cup pitted green olives

¾ cup granulated sugar

¾ cup Champagne vinegar

1 tablespoon juniper berries

Zest of 1 lemon

1. Place all the ingredients in a medium saucepan, bring to a boil, then remove from the heat.

2. Steep for 30 minutes, then strain through a fine-mesh strainer into a small bowl. Press to extract all the liquid.

3. The shrub will keep for 1 year in the refrigerator.

Oleo-Saccharum

Citrus shrubs use a technique that was frequently employed to make punches when such things were commonplace in English drinking life. The technique was reintroduced to modern cocktails in David Wondrich's book *Punch: The Delights (and Dangers) of the Flowing Bowl*.

Oleo-saccharum is a bastardized-Latinate term of art meaning "oily sugar," which sounds so icky you might as well put on some airs and use the Latin.

Once muddled together with citrus peels or zest, which will release the fruit's oils, the sugar will be fragrant with the citrus aroma, which will add a depth of flavor to a shrub that you wouldn't get from using sugar alone. You can also steal this technique the next time you make homemade lemonade.

The technique is pretty simple:

1. Using a vegetable peeler, remove the zest of your citrus fruit of choice in long strips, avoiding the bitter white pith.

2. Place the peels in a bowl and add your sugar of choice. Muddle the sugar and zest. If you don't have a cocktail muddler, use a ladle, wooden spoon, or pestle.

3. Cover the bowl with plastic wrap and leave it alone, at room temperature, for at least an hour, or even longer if you have the time. When you're ready, remove the peels from the bowl and discard, reserving the citrus-scented sugar.

Celery and Tarragon Shrub

I find this baffling, but celery seems to be a divisive vegetable. Many people seem to really hate it, but to me it's either too pale and boring to be offensive—like most of the stalks you'll find in the average grocery—or it's tart, pungent, and vivaciously green (and delicious!) like the stuff you can find at a farmers' market. Celery of either provenance will work in this recipe.

1 pound fresh celery

1 cup granulated sugar

1 cup apple cider vinegar

3 long stems fresh tarragon

1. Cut the celery stalks into 1-inch pieces.

2. Add the celery to a blender and cover with about ½ cup water.

3. Start the blender on low and, as the celery starts to get chopped, turn the speed up to puree. If the mixture seems thick and chunky, add a little more water.

4. Position a fine-mesh strainer over a small bowl and pour the mixture through it to remove the solids. Press or squeeze the celery puree to express the juice into the bowl.

5. Pour the celery juice into a jar or bottle. Add the sugar, vinegar, and tarragon, stems and all. Shake to combine.

6. Refrigerate for 2 days, shaking well each day. Remove the tarragon stems and any loose leaves.

Passion Fruit *and* Lemon Shrub *with* Earl Grey Tea

Passion fruit—with its flavors of kiwi, lemon, and pineapple—tastes bright and tart and punchy. These flavors mesh well with Earl Grey, a black tea originally flavored with oil of bergamot, which is a type of orange. (Many Earl Grey teas now are artificially flavored, however.) I think the blend of lemon, bergamot, and passion fruit in this shrub works very well, with the tea providing a strong herbal, earthy note.

5 passion fruits

1 lemon

¾ cup granulated sugar

¾ cup white wine vinegar

2 tea bags Earl Grey tea, or 2 tablespoons loose tea

1. Halve each passion fruit and scoop the flesh into a bowl.

2. Zest the lemon peel into the same bowl, then juice the lemon into that bowl. Add the sugar. Mash the fruit and stir to combine.

3. Cover the bowl and refrigerate for up to 2 days.

4. The next day, in a nonreactive container, steep the Earl Grey in the white wine vinegar for 1 hour, and then strain. (Any longer, and the Earl Grey flavor might become overpowering.)

5. Position a fine-mesh strainer over a small bowl and pour the passion fruit mixture through it to remove the solids.

6. Strain the vinegar mixture, through the same mesh strainer, into the same bowl as the passion fruit syrup. Stir to combine.

7. Pour the vinegar mixture into a clean mason jar. Cap, shake well to incorporate any undissolved sugar, and leave in the refrigerator for a week before using.

8. The shrub will keep for 1 year in the refrigerator.

Peach *and* Raspberry Shrub *with* Cinnamon *and* Maple

Maple and cinnamon are a classic flavor pair, and they bring rich, warm-spice tastes and aromas to the bright fruitiness of peaches and raspberries. The turbinado helps back up the deep flavors of the maple syrup. I grew up eating cinnamon-maple oatmeal from those little paper packets, and so this recipe carries the comfort of nostalgia.

4 ripe peaches (about 1½ pounds), pitted and cut into chunks

½ cup raspberries

½ cup pure maple syrup

¼ cup turbinado sugar

1 tablespoon freshly squeezed lemon juice

1 teaspoon ground cinnamon

¾ cup white wine vinegar

1. Combine the peaches, raspberries, maple syrup, turbinado sugar, lemon juice, and cinnamon in a medium saucepan. Cook over medium heat, stirring occasionally, until the mixture comes to a boil.

2. Lower the heat to medium-low. Cover the saucepan and allow to simmer, stirring occasionally, until the sugar dissolves and peaches can be mashed with a fork, about 10 minutes.

3. Remove from the heat and allow to cool.

4. Place a fine-mesh strainer over a small bowl and pour the fruit mixture through it to remove the solids.

5. Add the white wine vinegar.

6. Pour the vinegar mixture into a clean mason jar. Cap, shake well to incorporate any undissolved sugar, and leave in the refrigerator for a week before using.

7. The shrub will keep for 1 year in the refrigerator.

Peach *and* Black Tea Shrub

This shrub came about because I wanted to pay tribute to two mainstays of the American South: the peach tree and the sweet tea. (And of course peach tea is another southern mainstay.) Please make this when you can find great ripe peaches at a roadside farm stand or your own orchard.

- 6 ripe peaches (about 1½ pounds), pitted and cut into chunks
- 1 cup turbinado sugar
- 1 cup apple cider vinegar
- 1½ tablespoons loose-leaf black tea (or 2 tea bags)

1. Place the peaches and turbinado sugar in a medium bowl. Stir to combine.
2. Cover the bowl with plastic wrap and place in the refrigerator. Allow to macerate overnight.
3. Place a fine-mesh strainer over a small bowl and pour the peach mixture through it to remove the solids. Add the cider vinegar.
4. Pour the vinegar mixture into a clean mason jar. Cap, then shake well to incorporate any undissolved sugar.
5. Open the jar and add the tea (or tea bags). Cover and shake, then let sit at room temperature for 1 day. After 1 day, either strain off the liquid and discard the loose tea leaves, or remove the tea bags and gently squeeze the bags into the liquid before discarding them.
6. The shrub will keep for 1 year in the refrigerator.

Plum, Orange, *and* Clove Shrub

A versatile spice, cloves have a pungent, warm, spicy taste. Their flavor is sweet, penetrating, and astringent, with a mild bitterness that partners well with plums and oranges. This shrub is delicious just mixed with sparkling water (or sparkling wine), but it also goes great in cocktails starring rum or whiskey.

1½ pounds plums, pitted and crushed

Zest of 1 medium orange

1 tablespoon ground cloves

¾ cup turbinado sugar

¾ cup apple cider vinegar

1. Place the plums, orange zest, cloves, turbinado sugar, and cider vinegar in a medium bowl. Stir to combine.

2. Cover the bowl with plastic wrap and place in the refrigerator. Allow to macerate for up to 2 days.

3. Place a fine-mesh strainer over a small bowl and pour the plum mixture through it to remove the solids.

4. Pour the vinegar mixture into a clean mason jar. Cap, shake well to incorporate any undissolved sugar, and leave in the refrigerator for a week before using.

5. The shrub will keep for 1 year in the refrigerator.

Pear Shrub *with* Spiced Molasses Syrup

Sweet earthy pears and warm mulled-wine spices—combined with the deep rich taste of molasses—make this shrub a lovely winter delight. I've paired it later in the book with a crisp nutty sherry, but this would also mix well with fruit brandy.

PEAR SHRUB

- 3 medium pears, quartered (no need to peel, core, or seed)
- 1 cup apple cider vinegar

SPICED MOLASSES SYRUP

- ¾ cup molasses
- ¾ cup water
- 1 cinnamon stick
- 2 whole cloves
- 2 allspice berries

MAKE THE PEAR SHRUB

1. Using a box grater or a food processor, shred the pears.
2. Combine the shredded pears and cider vinegar in a nonreactive container. Cover and leave in a cool place on the countertop overnight.
3. Place a fine-mesh strainer over a bowl. Strain out the pear solids. Squeeze or press the mixture to remove any remaining liquid.
4. Pour the liquid into a clean mason jar or glass bottle, then add the spiced molasses syrup (directions follow).
5. Add a lid or cap, then shake well to combine. Place in the refrigerator.
6. The shrub will keep for 1 year in the refrigerator.

MAKE THE SPICED MOLASSES SYRUP

1. Combine the molasses and water in a small saucepan. Lightly crush the cinnamon stick, cloves, and allspice and add to the saucepan.

2. Warm over medium-low heat, stirring, until the molasses is fully dissolved in the water.

3. Allow a minimum of 10 minutes on the stove before removing from the heat.

4. Let the syrup cool.

5. Use a mesh strainer to remove the spices.

Pomegranate, Grapefruit, *and* Ginger Shrub

Wonderful pomegranate and juicy tart grapefruit marry with ginger in this fruity, spicy, and puckery shrub. Although there are various methods for extracting the juice from whole pomegranates, and I've tried them all in my time, I also find that using a bottled juice is perfectly fine. Just make sure it's pure pomegranate juice, and not mixed with other juices or sweeteners.

1½ cups unsweetened pomegranate juice

1 cup unsweetened grapefruit juice

2 tablespoons grated fresh ginger

¾ cup white wine vinegar

¾ cup granulated sugar

1. Combine all the ingredients in a large mason jar. Cover with the lid and stash in the fridge overnight.

2. Strain the mixture into a clean mason jar. Discard the ginger solids. Shake to fully dissolve any undissolved sugar.

3. The shrub will keep for 1 year in the refrigerator.

Papaya *and* Jalapeño Shrub

Papaya is a tropical and subtropical fruit, slightly sweet and somewhat musky, with a flavor similar to cantaloupe. Because papaya is sometimes used in salsas, I thought it would marry very well with jalapeño to create a savory shrub with subtle heat. Jalapeño, however, doesn't merely taste hot or spicy; it also has a crisp green bell pepper taste that's rather refreshing with the papaya.

2 papayas, peeled, seeded, and chopped

2 to 3 jalapeños, seeded and sliced thinly

1 cup apple cider vinegar

1 cup mild raw honey

1. Place all the ingredients in a medium saucepan, bring to a boil, and then remove from the heat.
2. Steep for 30 minutes, then strain through a fine-mesh strainer into a small bowl. Press to extract all the liquid.
3. The shrub will keep for 1 year in the refrigerator.

Rhubarb *and* Fennel Shrub

When I see rhubarb at the farmers' market, I usually get excited—it's one of the earliest offerings of spring, and it tells me that berries, peaches, and tomatoes are on their way. Rhubarb on its own is tart, woody, and puckery; in fact, many people find it too tart and woody, which is why it's most often eaten cooked in sweet preparations, such as pies and crumbles. Here, I've paired it with anise-hinted fennel, which melds nicely with tangy rhubarb. Light and delicate in flavor, and colored beautifully pink by the rhubarb, this shrub is tasty on its own or mixed with bubbly water. It's also great mixed into a tequila and soda.

1 pound rhubarb, leaves removed and discarded, stems diced

1 small fennel bulb, chopped, stalks and fronds saved for another use

1 cup granulated sugar

1 cup apple cider vinegar

1. Place the rhubarb, fennel, and sugar in a medium bowl and stir to combine.

2. Cover the bowl with plastic wrap and place in the fridge to macerate overnight.

3. Position a fine-mesh strainer over a small bowl and pour the mixture through it to remove the solids.

4. Combine the strained syrup with the cider vinegar. Whisk well to incorporate any undissolved sugar.

5. Pour the vinegar mixture into a clean mason jar. Cap, shake well to incorporate any undissolved sugar, and leave in the refrigerator for a week before using.

6. The shrub will keep for 1 year in the refrigerator.

Roasted Bell Pepper *and* Basil Shrub

Bell peppers are grassy and earthy, sweet and mildly herbal, with nearly no hint of peppery heat. Roasting them concentrates the sugars and sweetness, while also amping up their rich savory flavors. The basil in this is very subtle, but it sweetens the shrub and adds an earthy or grassy note. This would be a nice complement to tomato juice in a Bloody Mary.

3 red, orange, or yellow bell peppers, or a mix of the three colors

15 to 20 fresh basil leaves (about ½ ounce), bruised

¾ cup granulated sugar

¾ cup sherry vinegar

1. Preheat the oven to 500°F.
2. Place the whole peppers on a baking sheet and roast in the oven, turning at the 15- and 30-minute points, for a total of 45 minutes, or until the peppers are charred in spots and wrinkled.
3. Remove the peppers from the oven and immediately place in a heatproof bowl. Cover with plastic wrap or a plate so that the peppers can steam. Set aside for 30 minutes.
4. When the peppers are cool enough to handle, the skins should slip right off. Discard the skins, then remove the stems and seeds, and discard those as well. (Don't worry too much about the skins and seeds at this point. Discard what you can; you'll dispose of the rest in a later step.)
5. Place the roasted peppers, basil leaves, and sugar in a nonreactive container, cover with the sherry vinegar, and store in a cool, dark place overnight.

continues

6. Strain off the solids, reserving the liquid. Discard the leaves. Bottle or jar the liquid, cap, and shake well to combine. Leave in the fridge for 1 week before using.

7. The shrub will keep for 1 year in the refrigerator.

   NOTE: To bruise herbs, place the leaves in the palm of your hand. With your other hand, sharply slap the leaves. This releases essential oils trapped in the cells of the herb.

Roasted Pineapple *and* Lime Shrub *with* Ginger *and* Turmeric

Although I usually prefer fresh fruits in shrubs for their bright and vivid flavors, sometimes the flavor you get from cooking or roasting is unassailable, and such is the case with roasting pineapple, which concentrates and caramelizes the sugars in the fruit. The ginger and turmeric play off this to delicious effect, bringing their sharp pungent earthiness to jammy roasted fruit. Your grocery store might have precut pineapple in the produce section; feel free to use that if you want to save some effort cutting a whole pineapple.

2 cups cubed pineapple

½ cup apple cider vinegar

½ cup granulated sugar

¼ cup freshly squeezed lime juice

1 teaspoon grated fresh ginger

½ teaspoon ground turmeric

1. Preheat the oven to 450°F. Arrange the pineapple in a single layer on a foil-lined baking sheet. Roast in the oven for 15 to 20 minutes.

2. Place all the ingredients in a medium saucepan, bring to a boil, then remove from the heat.

3. Steep for 30 minutes, then strain through a fine-mesh strainer into a medium bowl. Press to extract all the liquid.

4. The shrub will keep for 1 year in the refrigerator.

Rosemary *and* Sage Shrub

Rosemary is a woodsy herb, with hints of pepper, mint, and citrus. Sage carries some of those same flavors, but with notes of eucalyptus. Together, they blend into a shrub that's bright and herbal. A shrub like this is great as a spritzer with soda or tonic water, but it's also ideal as an accent in gin or vodka drinks. Try a few drops stirred into a martini, a gimlet, or a gin and tonic!

6 sprigs rosemary

10 fresh sage leaves, bruised

1 cup white wine vinegar

1 cup granulated sugar

1. Place the rosemary and sage in a nonreactive container, cover with the white wine vinegar, and store in a cool, dark place overnight.

2. Strain off and discard the herbs, reserving the liquid. Bottle or jar the liquid. Add the sugar, lid it up, and shake well to combine. Leave in the fridge for 1 week.

3. The shrub will keep for 1 year in the refrigerator.

Strawberry *and* Habanero Shrub

Bringing more than just heat, habaneros also pack in sweet, floral, and fruity notes, which make them a great pairing with strawberries in this springtime shrub. I suggest one pepper for every two cups of strawberries, but obviously, you should feel free to adjust to meet your tolerance for *pow, biff,* and *zing*.

2 cups strawberries, hulled and quartered

1 habanero pepper, stem and seeds removed, chopped finely

½ cup granulated sugar

½ cup apple cider vinegar

1. Place all the ingredients in a medium bowl. Stir to combine.

2. Cover the bowl with plastic wrap and place in the refrigerator. Allow to macerate for up to 2 days.

3. Place a fine-mesh strainer over a small bowl and pour the mixture through it to remove the solids.

4. Pour the mixture into a clean mason jar. Cap, then shake well to incorporate any undissolved sugar.

5. The shrub will keep for 1 year in the refrigerator.

Strawberry *and* Fennel Seed Shrub

While researching this book, I had lunch at a local restaurant, where I tried a salad of strawberry, fennel, and arugula. The combination was surprisingly tasty; the slight licorice or anise notes of the fennel complemented well the sweetness of the berries. (I take a lot of shrub inspiration from salads, to be honest.) Although you can certainly use a sliced fennel bulb in this recipe (as I've done for other recipes in this book), I chose to keep it a little simpler and use fennel seed.

1½ cups (8 ounces) strawberries, hulled and quartered

½ cup granulated sugar

2 teaspoons fennel seeds

¾ cup apple cider vinegar

1. Place the strawberries and sugar in a medium bowl.
2. Use a mortar and pestle or a spice grinder to roughly crush the fennel seeds, or spread them on a cutting board and use the flat side of a knife to crush them.
3. Add the fennel seeds and cider vinegar to the bowl and stir to combine.
4. Place in the refrigerator. Allow to macerate for up to 2 days.
5. Position a fine-mesh strainer over a small bowl and pour the mixture through it to remove the solids.
6. Pour the mixture into a clean mason jar. Cap, shake well to incorporate any undissolved sugar, and leave in the refrigerator for a week before using.
7. The shrub will keep for 1 year in the refrigerator.

Tart Cherry *and* Sage Shrub

Some flavors have a surprising affinity. We use sage in sausage, or we think of it as a flavoring for poultry. We use it alongside the bird in Thanksgiving stuffing (or dressing, if you prefer). We think of gnocchi crisped up in sage-scented brown butter. But the earthiness of sage also partners well with juicy and such puckery fruits as tart cherry, pineapple, or citrus.

1½ pound tart cherries, lightly mashed (no need to pit them)

½ cup fresh sage leaves

1 cup apple cider vinegar

1 cup granulated sugar

1. Place all the ingredients in a medium bowl. Stir to combine. Cover with plastic wrap and place in the refrigerator. Allow to macerate for up to 2 days.

2. Position a fine-mesh strainer over a small bowl and pour the mixture through it to remove the solids.

3. Pour the mixture into a clean mason jar. Cap, shake well to incorporate any undissolved sugar, and leave in the refrigerator for a week before using.

4. The shrub will keep for 1 year in the refrigerator.

Roasted Sweet Potato Shrub *with* Turmeric *and* Garam Masala

A shrub that's savory, earthy, sweet, and influenced by South Asian spices, this recipe calls for roasting the sweet potatoes until they're caramelized and then seasoning the shrub with turmeric and garam masala. Turmeric is the rootstock of a plant in the ginger family, here used dried and finely ground. Garam masala is a blend of ground spices, consisting usually of cardamom, cinnamon, clove, and cumin.

2 large sweet potatoes, about 2 pounds

2 tablespoons olive oil

¾ cup granulated sugar

¾ cup apple cider vinegar

1 teaspoon ground turmeric

1 teaspoon garam masala

1. Preheat the oven to 375°F. Rub the sweet potatoes with the olive oil. Line a baking sheet with foil. Add the sweet potatoes, cover tightly with more foil, and roast in the oven for about 1 hour 15 minutes, or until you can easily pierce them with a fork. Remove from the oven and allow to thoroughly cool.

2. Use a spoon to scoop the sweet potato flesh into a mason jar. Add the remaining ingredients, lid up, and shake to combine. Leave in the fridge to combine the flavors overnight.

3. Position a fine-mesh strainer over a small bowl and pour the mixture through it to remove the solids.

4. Pour the vinegar mixture into a clean mason jar. Cap, shake well to incorporate any undissolved sugar, and leave in the refrigerator for a week before using.

5. The shrub will keep for 1 year in the refrigerator.

Tomato *and* Dill Shrub

Sweet, fruity shrubs are delightful, but a savory shrub can be just as tasty. This one marries summer tomatoes hot off the vine with fresh aromatic dill. Why the salt? To help draw out more tomato juice and punch up the savoriness just a tad.

2 pounds tomatoes, cored and quartered

1 tablespoon kosher salt

½ cup fresh dill

1 cup turbinado sugar

1 cup apple cider vinegar

1. Place all the ingredients in a medium bowl. Stir to combine. Cover with plastic wrap and leave in the refrigerator for 2 days.

2. Position a fine-mesh strainer over a small bowl and pour the mixture through it to remove the solids.

3. Pour the mixture into a clean mason jar. Cap, shake well to incorporate any undissolved sugar, and leave in the refrigerator for a week before using.

4. The shrub will keep for 1 year in the refrigerator.

Tomato, Cucumber, *and* Mint Shrub

Sometimes, when I'm developing these recipes, I'm trying to evoke a sense of seasonality, and this shrub is one of the best examples. I really want this one to scream SUMMER, with lush, juicy tomatoes, crisp and cooling cucumber, and peppery mint. The salt here is to draw out more juice from the tomatoes and also to punch up the savoriness of the shrub.

1 pound tomatoes, cored and quartered

1 large cucumber

½ cup fresh mint leaves

1 tablespoon kosher salt

1 cup turbinado sugar

1 cup apple cider vinegar

1. Place all the ingredients in a medium bowl. Stir to combine. Cover with plastic wrap and leave in the fridge for 2 days.

2. Position a fine-mesh strainer over a small bowl and pour the mixture through it to remove the solids.

3. Pour the mixture into a clean mason jar. Cap, shake well to incorporate any undissolved sugar, and leave in the refrigerator for a week before using.

4. The shrub will keep for 1 year in the refrigerator.

Watermelon, Cucumber, *and* Cilantro Shrub

A great cooling quencher for a hot day, this shrub combines watermelon and cucumber with cilantro for a nice grassy, herbal note. I don't know why, but I've never really liked melon; however, I can drink this all day every day. I've balanced apple cider vinegar with white wine vinegar to give this a brighter taste and let the main ingredients shine through more. If you can find precut watermelon, feel free to use that.

1½ **cups cubed and seeded watermelon**

1 **large cubed cucumber**

1 **cup granulated sugar**

1 **cup fresh cilantro leaves**

½ **cup white wine vinegar**

½ **cup apple cider vinegar**

1. Combine the watermelon and cucumber in a blender. Blend until pureed.
2. Press the puree through a fine-mesh strainer into a medium bowl.
3. Combine the puree (including any solids that passed through the strainer), sugar, cilantro, and both vinegars in a jar. Lid up, shake very well to combine, and leave in the refrigerator for 2 days.
4. Position a fine-mesh strainer over a small bowl and pour the mixture through to remove the solids.
5. Whisk the mixture well to incorporate any undissolved sugar.
6. Rinse the jar. Then, return the double-strained mixture to its jar, cap, and shake well to incorporate any remaining undissolved sugar. Leave in the refrigerator for a week before using.
7. The shrub will keep for 1 year in the refrigerator.

Yuzu *and* Matcha Shrub

Yuzu is a citrus fruit, similar to a clementine, that originated in China and Tibet. The flavor is similar to that of grapefruit or mandarin oranges. Matcha is a powdered form of green tea, ground to a fine consistency. Owing to the delicacy of these two flavors, I opted for honey and rice vinegar, so as to not overpower them. You could, if you wish, use white wine vinegar in place of the rice vinegar, and even granulated sugar in place of the honey.

6 large yuzu, juiced (should yield about ¼ cup juice), plus the peels

¼ cup honey

½ cup rice vinegar

2 tablespoons matcha tea powder

1. Combine the yuzu juice, peels, honey, and rice vinegar in a medium saucepan, bring to a boil, and then remove from the heat.

2. Steep for 30 minutes, then strain through a fine-mesh strainer into a small bowl. Press to extract all the liquid.

3. Add the matcha tea powder and transfer the mixture to a jar. Shake to combine, then leave in the refrigerator for 2 days to allow to fully blend.

4. The shrub will keep for 1 year in the refrigerator.

NOTE: If you want to "cheat," you can find yuzu vinegars in specialty stores or online. Some are presweetened with honey, in which case, simply add the matcha tea powder to taste and shake to combine.

COCKTAILS

Autumnal Bloody Mary

I've taken a traditional Bloody Mary in a slightly autumnal direction with Apple Horseradish Shrub, though a number of other shrubs in the book would go well with tomato juice in this cocktail. The herbal shrubs, such as Basil (page 48), Lavender (page 86), or Rosemary and Sage (page 112), would work well, especially if you wanted a faux-Italian spin using the Basil Shrub. The Cucumber, Cilantro, and Coriander Shrub (page 71) would make a fun Bloody Mary, as would the Tomato and Dill Shrub (page 119).

4 ounces Apple and Horseradish Shrub (page 44)

2 ounces vodka, gin, or aquavit (or omit, for a mocktail)

2 ounces tomato juice

1 teaspoon soy sauce

1 teaspoon garlic powder

1 teaspoon onion powder

4 dashes Angostura bitters

1. Combine all the ingredients in an ice-filled mixing glass. Take another glass, or the tin of a cocktail shaker, and gently pour the contents—ice and all—back and forth between the two vessels until the drink is well chilled.

2. Strain into an ice-filled collins glass.

Bowie's Buck

A buck is a cocktail made of ginger beer, a spirit of some type, and citrus juice. (One variation on a buck is a mule, which usually contains vodka and is named for the Moscow Mule.) This variant calls for gin and pineapple shrub. The piney qualities of the gin complement the toasty-tasting roasted pineapple.

2 ounces London dry gin

1 ounce freshly squeezed lime juice

¾ ounce Roasted Pineapple and Lime Shrub with Ginger and Turmeric (page 111)

Ginger beer

Lime wedges for garnish

1. Pour the gin, lime juice, and shrub into an ice-filled copper mug.
2. Add the ginger beer and stir.
3. Garnish with the lime wedges.

Bourbon Peach Tea Cooler

This was inspired by flavors from the American South: sweet tea, bourbon whiskey, and peaches. A pitcher of this should make 12 servings. If you'll need more for your picnic or barbecue, just double or triple everything.

3 cups Peach and Black Tea Shrub (page 100)

1 cup bourbon (I used Maker's Mark brand)

1 cup water

Peach slices for garnish

1. Combine the shrub and bourbon, along with the water, in a 1-gallon pitcher and stir briskly.

2. Serve in highball glasses over ice and garnish with peach slices.

    NOTE: For one individual serving, combine 2 ounces of Peach and Black Tea Shrub, ¾ ounce of bourbon, and ¾ ounce of water in a highball glass over ice.

Chamomile *and* Pear Toddy

A toddy is usually a hot drink consisting of liquor, water, sugar, and spices. Because toddies are traditionally served as nightcaps, it seemed obvious to use a shrub containing chamomile, which is thought to promote sleep. Choose gin if you want to add another herbal element to the drink, and vodka if you'd rather let the shrub shine through. Of course, you can also enjoy it without the booze.

1½ ounces vodka or London dry gin (omit for nonalcoholic toddy)

3 ounces Chamomile, Pear, and Lavender Shrub (page 132)

¼ ounce freshly squeezed Meyer lemon juice

2 teaspoons honey

¼ cup boiling water

1 lemon slice for garnish

1. Combine the vodka or gin, shrub, Meyer lemon juice, and honey in a 6-ounce mug. Top with the hot water and stir until the honey is dissolved. Garnish with the lemon slice.

Fruited Gin *and* Tonic

When you just want a refreshing pick-me-up, nothing can approach a G-n-T. Though you cannot improve upon perfection, you can change its pace a bit and pop in a bit of shrub. I chose the Pomegranate, Grapefruit, and Ginger Shrub (page 104) here, but you can use almost anything.

2 ounces London dry gin, such as Tanqueray brand

1 ounce Pomegranate, Grapefruit, and Ginger Shrub (page 104)

3 ounces tonic water

1. Pour the gin and shrub over ice in a tall glass. Stir to mix thoroughly.
2. Add the tonic water, then stir *gently* to mix without disturbing the bubbles.

Good Gourd, Margarita!

Watermelons and cucumbers are both members of the Cucurbitaceae plant family, also known as cucurbits or gourds. The shrub in this is cooling and mellow and rounds out the agave grassiness of the tequila.

Lime wedge

Coarse sea salt

2 ounces tequila blanco

1 ounce Watermelon, Cucumber, and Cilantro Shrub (page 123)

½ ounce orange liqueur (such as Cointreau)

½ ounce freshly squeezed lime juice

1. Rim a cocktail glass: Rub the lime wedge along the rim of a chilled cocktail glass. Dip the glass into the sea salt to coat the edge. (Alternatively—and my own preference—you can coat half the rim in salt and leave the other half uncoated. That way, not every sip will be salty.)

2. Combine all the other ingredients in an ice-filled cocktail shaker. Shake until well chilled.

3. Strain into the prepared cocktail glass.

   NOTE: If desired, you can prepare the cocktail glass in advance and chill it in the freezer until ready to mix the cocktail.

Olive Shrub Dirty Martini

I have a confession: I love a dirty martini. I know, I know, cocktail geeks aren't supposed to love them. We're all supposed to prefer 50-50 blends of London dry gin and expensive French vermouth. Or we're told we need to go the opposite direction and embrace a very cold glass of icy gin straight from the freezer with the merest breath of vermouth. And I do love those things. It's just I also enjoy a briny martini, too. So much of what I want at any martini moment depends on my circumstances and my mood. If you love an olive-forward martini, too, give this a try!

2 ounces dry gin or vodka

½ ounce dry vermouth

¼ ounce Olive, Lemon, and Juniper Shrub (page 93)

Olive or lemon twist for garnish

1. Combine the gin, vermouth, and shrub in an ice-filled mixing glass, then stir.
2. Strain into a chilled cocktail glass.
3. Garnish with an olive or lemon twist.

Johnny After a Fashion

This cocktail is simply an old-fashioned, gussied up with a bit of shrub (instead of simple syrup or sugar) and substituting apple brandy for the traditional bourbon or rye whiskey. I prefer a 100-proof bottling of apple brandy, such as Laird's, for this.

2 ounces apple brandy

½ ounce Fig and Green Anise Shrub (page 74)

3 dashes black walnut or Angostura bitters

1. Combine all the ingredients in an ice-filled mixing glass, then stir.
2. Strain into a rocks glass filled with ice.

Nor'easter Winter Punch

A delicious, warming punch for fall or winter holiday parties. The combination of apple brandy and dark rum is surprisingly tasty on its own; the way these aged spirits intermingle is really nice, but add the Cranberry and Pine Needle Shrub (page 68), and the punch takes on another layer of good cheer.

- 2 cups apple brandy
- 1 cup dark rum (Smith & Cross brand, if you can find it, or Planteray Original Dark; do not use spiced rum for this)
- 1 cup Cranberry and Pine Needle Shrub (page 68)
- 2 cups fresh apple cider
- 3 cinnamon sticks

1. Combine all the ingredients in a large pitcher.
2. Serve over ice in individual punch mugs.

Pinenana Frozen Daiquiri

In recent years, craft-cocktail bars around the world have rediscovered the joy of the large-batch frozen drink, or booze slushy. I figure, why shouldn't we get in on the fun, too? This is delicious, but be careful: it'll sneak up on you before you know it.

- 4 ounces white rum
- 2 ounces Banana and Pineapple Shrub with Nutmeg (page 50)
- 2 ounces full-fat coconut milk
- 1 ounce freshly squeezed lime juice
- 1 ounce dry orange curaçao
- 3 cups crushed ice

1. Combine the rum, shrub, coconut milk, lime juice, curaçao, and crushed ice in a blender, then blend. Pour into chilled glasses.

Plum Shrub Sidecar

The sidecar is a drink of some distinction, one of the most enduring cocktails in the classic canon. Although its specific provenance is as yet unknown, the drink first appears in two cocktail manuals published in London in 1922, and one of those books cites its origins as stemming from the South of France, possibly Cannes. Nevertheless, during the 1920s, the sidecar achieved great fame in bars in both Europe and New York City.

    I've paired this evergreen classic with a shrub of plum, orange, and cloves, all flavors that meld well with brandy. A common way to serve the sidecar is with the rim of the glass frosted with superfine sugar; tastes vary, but I prefer the drink without the added sweetener.

1½ ounces cognac

¾ ounce Cointreau

½ ounce Plum, Orange, and Clove Shrub (page 101)

¼ ounce freshly squeezed lemon juice

1. Combine all the ingredients in an ice-filled cocktail shaker. Shake well.
2. Strain into a chilled cocktail glass.

Remember the Day We...

The classic cocktail Remember the Maine first appeared in the travelogue *The Gentleman's Companion*, by Charles H. Baker, published in 1939. The cocktail seems to have arisen in Havana, and the name references the Spanish-American War. But enough history... the original drink calls for an absinthe rinse in the serving glass, along with rye whiskey, vermouth, and cherry brandy. In this case, we'll swap in a bit of shrub.

½ teaspoon absinthe

2 ounces rye whiskey

¾ ounce sweet vermouth

¼ ounce Tart Cherry and Sage Shrub (page 117)

Brandied cherry for garnish

1. Pour the absinthe into a chilled cocktail glass. Swirl to coat and then discard the excess.
2. Combine the whiskey, vermouth, and shrub in a mixing glass filled with ice and stir until well chilled.
3. Strain into the prepared cocktail glass.
4. Garnish with the brandied cherry.

Rosie Collins

A Tom Collins is a long drink of gin, lemon juice, and simple syrup, topped with soda water, and garnished with a lemon wheel. Tom's granddad, the John Collins, dates back to something like the 1830s (it's hard to be precise), making it one of the oldest families of cocktails still popular today. (Not that I knew this when I was drinking them clandestinely at the age of 15, pretending they were Sprite.) For this variation, I've added a spot of Grape and Rosemary Shrub (page 80) to liven up the drink, since the classic Tom Collins, to my taste now, is a little bland.

2 ounces London dry gin

¾ ounce Grape and Rosemary Shrub (page 80)

¼ ounce freshly squeezed lemon juice

Soda water

Lemon wheel for garnish

1. Combine the gin, shrub, and lemon juice in a tall glass filled with ice. Stir until well chilled.

2. Top with soda water and garnish the rim of the glass with the lemon wheel.

Sherry Baby Cobbler

A cobbler is one of the oldest cocktails that remains in somewhat active circulation. You can't find them everywhere, unfortunately, but the places that do make them are generally committed to making them correctly—and deliciously. But when the julep and the collins were scrabbling their way to the top of the 19th-century drinks heap, the cobbler was right alongside them. A cobbler is nothing more than wine (often fortified, such as sherry) shaken with sugar and ice, and garnished with berries or fruit.

4 ounces amontillado sherry

1 ounce Pear Shrub with Spiced Molasses Syrup (page 102)

Berries, fresh mint, or citrus peels for garnish

1. Stir the sherry and shrub together in a tall glass. Add ice and stir again.
2. Add your choice of garnish and drink through a straw.

Smashed Hippopotamus

This cocktail kinda-sorta takes a margarita and tosses it in the air a few times and takes it for a spin around the block before serving it to you over ice in a tall glass. What's with the name? I dunno, it amused me at the time.

1½ ounces blanco tequila

¾ ounce lime juice

½ ounce Celery and Tarragon Shrub (page 95)

½ ounce pineapple juice

2 teaspoons agave nectar

1. Combine all the ingredients in an ice-filled cocktail shaker. Shake well.

2. Strain into a tall glass filled with ice.

Strawbanero Highball

This highball blends sweet, jammy strawberries with zippy habaneros and cooling mint. Pour it tall and sip it slowly on a lovely late spring day.

HIGHBALL

- 1½ ounces Strawberry and Habanero Shrub (page 113)
- 1½ ounces vodka (omit for nonalcoholic mocktail)
- ¼ ounce freshly squeezed lemon juice
- ¼ ounce mint simple syrup (recipe follows)
- Club soda
- Fresh mint for garnish

MINT SIMPLE SYRUP

- 1 cup water
- 1 cup granulated sugar
- 1 cup fresh mint leaves

MAKE THE HIGHBALL

1. Combine the shrub, vodka, lemon juice, and mint simple syrup in an ice-filled cocktail shaker. Shake well, then strain into an ice-filled highball glass.
2. Top with club soda and stir gently to combine without disturbing bubbles.
3. Garnish with fresh mint.

MAKE THE MINT SIMPLE SYRUP

1. Combine the water, sugar, and mint leaves in a small saucepan. Bring to a boil over medium heat, stirring until the sugar dissolves. Simmer for 1 minute; remove from the heat and let the syrup steep for about 30 minutes.
2. Strain into a glass jar to remove the mint leaves. Discard the leaves. Allow the syrup to cool and then refrigerate.

Tipsy Rabbit

The Tipsy Rabbit would be a great drink for guests: the shrub is bright orange, so the cocktail carries a bright and festive appeal. The meld of gin, carrots, and ginger is surprisingly tasty. There's not much to say about this savory sipper except Cheers!

2 ounces London dry gin, such as Tanqueray brand

1 ounce Carrot, Apple, and Caraway Shrub (page 61)

¾ ounce ginger liqueur

1. Combine all the ingredients in an ice-filled cocktail shaker. Shake well.
2. Strain into a chilled cocktail glass.

Yuzu Matcha Sour

The sour is simply a cocktail made of spirits, citrus juice, and a sweetening agent. This sweetener could be sugar, it could be simple syrup, it could be triple sec or another sweet liqueur. The margarita is a sour made of tequila, lime, and either triple sec or agave nectar. The daiquiri has rum, lime, and sugar. The Cosmo is citrus vodka, lime, Cointreau, and cranberry. You get the idea. Some sours, such as this one, also contain egg white. In most cases, most of the time, most of the eggs you buy in the store are safe to use in raw preparations. If you don't want the risk, you can use pasteurized egg whites from a carton.

2 ounces Suntory Whisky Toki

½ ounce Yuzu and Matcha Shrub (page 124)

¼ ounce freshly squeezed lemon juice

½ ounce raw egg white

Angostura bitters for garnish

1. Combine the whisky, shrub, lemon juice, and egg white in a shaker and dry shake (without ice) vigorously for 10 seconds to fully combine the egg white with the other ingredients.
2. Add ice cubes and shake again until well chilled.
3. Strain into a chilled cocktail glass.
4. Garnish by dashing about 10 drops of Angostura onto the foamy surface of the cocktail.

MOCKTAILS

Agua Fresca

A common use of shrubs—possibly the most common—is to pour them over ice in a glass and top with soda or tonic water. Agua fresca is similar, in that you dilute the shrub with water, but the main differences are, first, that the water is still instead of bubbly; and second, that you use less shrub.

Aguas frescas are lightly flavored beverages of fruits, seeds, flowers, grains, or leaves, sweetened with sugar, possibly mixed with a bit of lime juice to add tartness, and finally stirred into a whole lot of water. Aguas frescas are meant to refresh and rehydrate, not provide a flavor bomb, and so the flavor is usually kept light. In Mexico and other Latin American countries, they're prepared in great glass containers, kept cold, and sold by street vendors.

Traditional ingredients include cantaloupe, watermelon, lime, hibiscus flowers, guava, and tamarind. Horchata is another type of agua fresca, made with ground rice mixed with cinnamon and sweetened water.

BASIC RECIPE

4 cups filtered water

1 cup shrub of choice

1. Combine the water and shrub in a large pitcher.
2. Pour over ice in a tall glass.

Chocolate Coconut Lemongrass Soda

A delicious sweet soda for a relaxing afternoon, this pairs coconut with an obvious partner, rich chocolate.

2 ounces Coconut and Lemongrass Shrub (page 65)

1 ounce chocolate syrup

Soda water

1. Combine all the ingredients in an ice-filled glass. Stir gently to blend. Sip through a straw.

Holiday Cran-Orange Spritzer

A light, simple nonalcoholic drink for your holiday gatherings, this spritzer brings flavors of fall and winter to the festive table.

2 ounces Cranberry and Pine Needle Shrub (page 68)

3 ounces orange-flavored sparkling water

1. Combine the ingredients in a glass over ice, and stir lightly. Sip through a straw.

Honeyfig Julep

The mint julep is one of the oldest mixed drinks on record in the United States, but the origins of the word *julep* date back even further. In fact, the julep has its origins in Persia, from around the same time as the Persians were making sakanjabīn and oxymel. The word *julep* derives from the Persian *gûl-ab* (rose water). In this alcohol-free julep, the sweet but robust flavor of the fig replaces the bourbon usually found in a julep.

2 ounces Honeydew, Fig, and Mint Shrub (page 85)

8 to 10 fresh mint leaves

Mint sprigs for garnish

1. Place the shrub at the bottom of a julep cup or tall glass. Add the mint leaves and gently bruise with a wooden muddler or wooden spoon. Be sure to swab the sides of the vessel with the mint's aromatic oils.

2. Half-fill the vessel with crushed ice and stir to combine. Fill with more crushed ice and stir until the outside of the vessel frosts. Add more crushed ice if needed to refill.

3. Garnish with a generous amount of fresh mint.

Nanacolada

Although we think of piña colada as a rum-based boozy drink, it actually has its origins as a nonalcoholic drink from Cuba, made of sweetened pineapple juice and coconut water. Eventually, someone had the idea to spike it with rum, and the version we know today—rummy and laced with thicker, sweeter cream of coconut instead of coconut water—arose in Puerto Rico somewhere around the mid-1950s or early 1960s.

4 ounces Roasted Pineapple and Lime Shrub with Ginger and Turmeric (page 111)

4 ounces Coco López brand cream of coconut

Pineapple slices for garnish

Maraschino cherries for garnish

1. Combine the shrub, cream of coconut, and 3 cups of ice in a blender. Process until smooth. Add more ice, if necessary, to make it frostier.

2. Pour into tall glasses and garnish with pineapple slices and maraschino cherries.

Papaya Jalapeño Lassi

A lassi is a yogurt-based drink from the Punjab region of India. Sweet varieties made from mango and strawberries are popular, but the drink can also be served as a savory beverage, seasoned with salt and such spices as cumin or cardamom. This recipe makes enough for two servings.

1½ cups full-fat Greek yogurt

1 cup Papaya and Jalapeño Shrub (page 106)

1. Combine the yogurt, shrub, and ½ cup of ice cubes in a blender. Process until smooth. Add more ice, if necessary, to make it frostier. Pour into two tall glasses.

Zingy Ginger Mocktail

One for the ginger lovers everywhere.

2 ounces Mint and Ginger Shrub (page 92)

3 ounces ginger beer

1. Combine the ingredients in a glass over ice and stir lightly.

Acknowledgments

When this book opportunity arose, I needed to find a new photographer. My wife had photographed my previous books, but work and other obligations precluded her from doing so again. We're now in Baltimore, and so I started searching Instagram and other online resources to find someone local. In this way, I found the immensely talented Becca Maffet, from Terragold Photo, who shot everything you've seen in this book. Her work is lively and beautiful, and I could not be happier. Many thanks to you, Becca, and to your assistant, Kristen Murphy, for her skilled eye.

At Countryman Press, I'd like to thank my editor, Ann Treistman, for shepherding this book from concept to completion, as well as her team—Devon Zahn, Jess Murphy, Allison Chi, Raphael Geroni, Maya Goldfarb, Devorah Backman, and Zach Polendo. I also want to thank our copy editor, Iris Bass, and indexer, Elizabeth Parson, for their thoroughgoing work.

My agent, Vicky Bijur, deserves every ounce of gratitude I can muster for her grace, humor, and inimitable skill with a contract.

Finally, but certainly not least, Jen and the kids have been an endless source of encouragement and love as we've navigated these last 18 months. When I wrote my first book on this topic, *Shrubs*, back in 2013, my eldest was about to turn 2 and my youngest was in utero. Now they are a teen and tween, and I have no idea how that could have happened. You're the absolute best, and you make me happy every day.

Resources

SHRUB MAKERS

TAIT FARM FOODS, the folks who started the bottled shrub movement, are still going strong, with a line of over a dozen shrub flavors. Find them at taitfarmfoods.com.

BUG HILL FARM, in the Berkshires in Massachusetts, makes shrubs, conserves, and cordials from its berry farm. (www.bughillfarm.org)

SHRUBBLY, located in Vermont, markets canned shrubs in grocery stores and cafés on the US East Coast, though you can also order online. (shrubbly.com)

TWISTED BEVERAGE CO., in Minneapolis, offers bottled shrubs and flavored shots of apple cider vinegar, on its website at thetwistedshrub.com.

CRAFTED BRAND CO., in California, makes cocktail and mocktail mixers, shrubs, syrups, and bar condiments. Find them at www.craftedcocktails.com.

ELEMENT SHRUB, just outside Boston, makes a line of shrubs that they offer in stores and online at www.elementshrub.com.

If you prefer to shop local, of course, you might find a health-food store in your town that offers their own shrubs, or you might track some down at your nearby farmers' market!

VINEGARS

CHAPARRAL GARDENS, in California, makes a variety of balsamic and fruit vinegars. (www.chaparralgardens.com)

FIORE ARTISAN OLIVE OILS AND VINEGARS, in Maine, makes balsamic and other wine vinegars. Shop at fioreoliveoils.com.

AMERICAN VINEGAR WORKS, in Worcester, Massachusetts, offers a line of vinegars made from wine, cider, craft beer, rice wine, and mead. (americanvinegarworks.com)

Food Safety Tips

The following tips are adapted from "Preserving Food: Flavored Vinegars," a pamphlet from the National Center for Home Food Preservation (NCHFP) and the University of Georgia Cooperative Extension Service:

1. **PREPARE YOUR JARS OR BOTTLES.** The NCHFP suggests using only glass containers for storing vinegars. Wash them well and then add them carefully to a deep pot. Completely cover them with water, turn on the stove, and bring the water to a boil. Boil for 10 minutes. Remove the jars from the water, drain the water out of them, and fill while they're still warm.

2. **PREPARE YOUR FRUIT.** Prepare a sanitizing solution of vinegar and water. Add 1 tablespoon of distilled white vinegar to 6 cups of water. Soak the fruit in the solution for 10 minutes, rinse, and drain until mostly dry.

3. **PREPARE YOUR HERBS, IF YOU'RE FOLLOWING A RECIPE THAT CALLS FOR THEM.** Fresh herbs can attract microbes, so if you want to be as safe as possible, you might want to disinfect them. First, wash the herbs well and gently, so as not to damage them. Make a sanitizing solution of 1 teaspoon chlorine bleach to 6 cups of water. Dip the herbs in the sanitizing solution, rinse under cold water, and blot dry with paper towels.

Index

Note: Page references in *italics* indicate photographs.

Absinthe
    Remember the Day We . . ., 146
Agua Fresca, *158,* 159
Allspice, Apple, and Thyme Shrub, 45
Apple
    Carrot, and Caraway Shrub, *60,* 61
    and Horseradish Shrub, 44
    Thyme, and Allspice Shrub, 45
Apple brandy
    Johnny After a Fashion, *138, 139*
    Nor'easter Winter Punch, *140,* 141
Apricot, Basil, and Balsamic Shrub, *46,* 47

Banana
    and Coconut Shrub with Cinnamon and Clove, 49
    and Pineapple Shrub with Nutmeg, 50, *51*
Basil
    Apricot, and Balsamic Shrub, *46,* 47
    and Mango Shrub, 88
    and Roasted Bell Pepper Shrub, *108,* 109–110
    Shrub, 48
Berries, 29. *See also specific berries*
Blackberry and Black Pepper Shrub, 56
Bloody Mary, Autumnal, 128
Blueberry, Cinnamon, and Clove Shrub, 54, *55*
Bottled juices, 33
Bourbon Peach Tea Cooler, *130,* 131

Bowie's Buck, 129
Brandy. *See* Apple brandy

Cantaloupe, Fennel, and Star Anise Shrub, 57
Caraway, Carrot, and Apple Shrub, *60,* 61
Carrot
    Apple, and Caraway Shrub, *60,* 61
    and Fenugreek Shrub, 59
Celery and Tarragon Shrub, 95
Chamomile, Pear, and Lavender Shrub, 58
Cherry
    and Cocoa Shrub with Cinnamon, 66
    Tart, and Sage Shrub, *116,* 117
Chocolate
    Cherry and Cocoa Shrub with Cinnamon, 66
    Coconut Lemongrass Soda, 160, *161*
Cilantro
    Cucumber, and Coriander Shrub, *70* , 71
    Lime, and Jalapeño Shrub, 62, *63*
    Watermelon, and Cucumber Shrub, *122,* 123
Cinnamon, Blueberry, and Clove Shrub, 54, *55*
Citrus fruits, 30. *See also specific citrus fruits*
    Oleo-Saccharum, 94
Clove
    Blueberry, and Cinnamon Shrub, 54, *55*
    Fig, and Vanilla Shrub, 73
    Plum, and Orange Shrub, 101

Cobbler, Sherry Baby, 148, *149*
Cocktails, list of, 7
Coconut, 33
    and Banana Shrub with Cinnamon and Clove, 49
    Lemongrass Chocolate Soda, 160, *161*
    and Lemongrass Shrub, *64,* 65
    Nanacolada, 165
    Pinenana Frozen Daiquiri, 142, *143*
Coffee Shrub with Raspberry and Thyme, 67
Cognac
    Plum Shrub Sidecar, *144,* 145
Collins, Rosie, 147
Coriander, Cucumber, and Cilantro Shrub, *70* , 71
Cranberry
    Holiday Cran-Orange Spritzer, *162,* 163
    and Pine Needle Shrub, 68, *69*
Cucumber
    Cilantro, and Coriander Shrub, *70* , 71
    Tomato, and Mint Shrub, 120, *121*
    Watermelon, and Cilantro Shrub, *122,* 123

Daiquiri, Pinenana Frozen, 142, *143*
Dill and Tomato Shrub, 119

Fennel
    Cantaloupe, and Star Anise Shrub, 57
    and Rhubarb Shrub, 107

Seed and Strawberry Shrub, 114, *115*
and Tarragon Shrub, 72
Fenugreek and Carrot Shrub, 59
Fig
    Clove, and Vanilla Shrub, 73
    and Green Anise Shrub, 74
    Honeydew, and Mint Shrub, *84,* 85
Fire Cider Shrub, 75–76, *77*
Fruits, 29–33, 36. *See also specific fruits*
Fruit vegetables, 33
Fruit vinegars, note on, 40

Gin
    Autumnal Bloody Mary, 128
    Bowie's Buck, 129
    Chamomile and Pear Toddy, 132, *133*
    Olive Shrub Dirty Martini, 137
    Rosie Collins, 147
    Tipsy Rabbit, *152,* 153
    and Tonic, Fruited, *134,* 135
Ginger
    Blood Orange, and Old Bay Shrub, 53
    Fire Cider Shrub, 75–76, *77*
    and Green Tea Shrub, *78,* 79
    and Mint Shrub, 92
    Pomegranate, and Grapefruit Shrub, 104, *105*
    Tipsy Rabbit, *152,* 153
Ginger beer
    Bowie's Buck, 129
    Zingy Ginger Mocktail, *168,* 169
Grape and Rosemary Shrub, 80
Grapefruit, Pomegranate, and Ginger Shrub, 104, *105*
Green Anise and Fig Shrub, 74

Herbal teas, 36
Herbs, 33, 36. *See also specific herbs*
Hibiscus Shrub, 82, *83*
Highball, Strawbanero, 151
Honeydew
    Fig, and Mint Shrub, *84,* 85
    Honeyfig Julep, 164

Horseradish
    and Apple Shrub, 44
    Fire Cider Shrub, 75–76, *77*

Julep, Honeyfig, 164
Juniper, Olive, and Lemon Shrub, 93

Lassi, Papaya Jalapeño, 166, *167*
Lavender
    Chamomile, and Pear Shrub, 58
    Shrub, 86, *87*
Lemon
    Fire Cider Shrub, 75–76, *77*
    Meyer, and Za'atar Shrub, *90,* 91
    Olive, and Juniper Shrub, 93
    and Passion Fruit Shrub with Earl Grey Tea, 96, *97*
Lemongrass and Coconut Shrub, *64,* 65
Lime
    Cilantro, and Jalapeño Shrub, 62, *63*
    and Roasted Pineapple Shrub with Ginger and Turmeric, 111

Mango
    and Basil Shrub, 88
    and Passion Fruit Shrub with Black Pepper and Mint, 89
Margarita, Good Gourd!, 136
Martini, Olive Shrub Dirty, 137
Mint
    and Ginger Shrub, 92
    Honeydew, and Fig Shrub, *84,* 85
    Honeyfig Julep, 164
    Strawbanero Highball, 151
    Tomato, and Cucumber Shrub, 120, *121*
    Zingy Ginger Mocktail, *168,* 169
Mocktails, list of, 7
Molasses Syrup, Spiced, Pear Shrub with, 102–103

Nanacolada, 165
Nor'easter Winter Punch, *140,* 141

Oleo-Saccharum, 94
Olive
    Lemon, and Juniper Shrub, 93
    Shrub Dirty Martini, 137
Orange
    Blood, Ginger, and Old Bay Shrub, 53
    -Cran Spritzer, Holiday, *162,* 163
    Plum, and Clove Shrub, 101
Orange curaçao
    Pinenana Frozen Daiquiri, 142, *143*
Orange liqueur
    Good Gourd, Margarita!, 136
    Plum Shrub Sidecar, *144,* 145

Papaya
    Jalapeño Lassi, 166, *167*
    and Jalapeño Shrub, 106
Passion Fruit
    and Lemon Shrub with Earl Grey Tea, 96, *97*
    and Mango Shrub with Black Pepper and Mint, 89
Peach
    and Black Tea Shrub, 100
    Bourbon Tea Cooler, *130,* 131
    and Raspberry Shrub with Cinnamon and Maple, *98,* 99
Pear
    Chamomile, and Lavender Shrub, 58
    Shrub with Spiced Molasses Syrup, 102–103
Pepper(s)
    Cilantro, Lime, and Jalapeño Shrub, 62, *63*
    Habanero, Watermelon, and Thyme Shrub, 81
    Papaya and Jalapeño Shrub, 106
    Roasted Bell, and Basil Shrub, *108,* 109–110
    Strawberry and Habanero Shrub, 113

Pineapple
    and Banana Shrub with Nutmeg, 50, *51*
    Nanacolada, 165
    Roasted, and Lime Shrub with Ginger and Turmeric, 111
    Smashed Hippopotamus, 150
Pine Needle and Cranberry Shrub, 68, *69*
Plum, Orange, and Clove Shrub, 101
Pome fruit, 29–30
Pomegranate, Grapefruit, and Ginger Shrub, 104, *105*

Raspberry
    and Peach Shrub with Cinnamon and Maple, *98*, 99
    and Thyme, Coffee Shrub with, 67
Remember the Day We . . ., 146
Rhubarb and Fennel Shrub, 107
Rosemary
    and Grape Shrub, 80
    and Sage Shrub, 112
Rosie Collins, 147
Rum
    Nor'easter Winter Punch, *140*, 141
    Pinenana Frozen Daiquiri, 142, *143*

Sage
    and Rosemary Shrub, 112
    and Tart Cherry Shrub, *116*, 117
Sherry Baby Cobbler, 148, *149*
Shrubs
    definition, 17
    evolution of term, 18
    flavor pairings and substitutions, 12–15
    history of, 9–10, 18–25
    hot and cold processes, 27–28
    ingredients for, 29–40
    list of recipes, 6–7
    safety tips, 28
    storing, 28
    tools for, 28
Sidecar, Plum Shrub, *144*, 145
Smashed Hippopotamus, 150
Soda, Chocolate Coconut Lemongrass, 160, *161*
Sour, Yuzu Matcha, 154, *155*
Spices, 33
Spritzer, Holiday Cran-Orange, *162*, 163
Star Anise, Cantaloupe, and Fennel Shrub, 57
Stone fruits, 30
Strawberry
    and Fennel Seed Shrub, 114, *115*
    and Habanero Shrub, 113
    Strawbanero Highball, 151
Sugars
    Oleo-Saccharum, 94
    types of, 38
Sweeteners, 38–39
Sweet Potato, Roasted, Shrub with Turmeric and Garam Masala, 118

Tarragon
    and Celery Shrub, 95
    and Fennel Shrub, 72
Tea, 36
    Black, and Peach Shrub, 100
    Earl Grey, Passion Fruit and Lemon Shrub with, 96, *97*
    Green, and Ginger Shrub, *78*, 79
    Yuzu and Matcha Shrub, 124, *125*
Tequila
    Good Gourd, Margarita!, 136
    Smashed Hippopotamus, 150
Thyme
    Apple, and Allspice Shrub, 45
    Habanero, and Watermelon Shrub, 81
    and Raspberry, Coffee Shrub with, 67
Tipsy Rabbit, *152*, 153
Toddy, Chamomile and Pear, 132, *133*
Tomato
    Autumnal Bloody Mary, 128
    Cucumber, and Mint Shrub, 120, *121*
    and Dill Shrub, 119
Tropical fruits, 30
Turmeric
    Fire Cider Shrub, 75–76, *77*

Vanilla, Fig, and Clove Shrub, 73
Vegetables, 33, 36. *See also specific vegetables*
Vermouth
    Olive Shrub Dirty Martini, 137
    Remember the Day We . . ., 146
Vinegars, 39–40
Vodka
    Autumnal Bloody Mary, 128
    Chamomile and Pear Toddy, 132, *133*
    Olive Shrub Dirty Martini, 137
    Strawbanero Highball, 151

Watermelon
    Cucumber, and Cilantro Shrub, *122*, 123
    Habanero, and Thyme Shrub, 81
Whiskey
    Remember the Day We . . ., 146
    Yuzu Matcha Sour, 154, *155*

Yogurt
    Papaya Jalapeño Lassi, 166, *167*
Yuzu
    and Matcha Shrub, 124, *125*
    Matcha Sour, 154, *155*

Za'atar and Meyer Lemon Shrub, *90*, 91